I0098599

FAITH IS WORTH FIGHTING FOR

Second Edition

nt © 2020 by Stephanie M. White

N: 978-0-9828743-0-1

All rights reserved. No part of this book may be reproduced or transmitted in any form or by any means, electronic or mechanical, including photocopying, recording, or by any information storage and retrieval system, without permission in writing from the copyright owner.

This book was printed in the United States of America.

To contact the author:

https://whitestephanie83.wixsite.com/heavenonearthforyou

Life Under Divine Influence

God's Truth About Law and Grace

Stephanie M. White

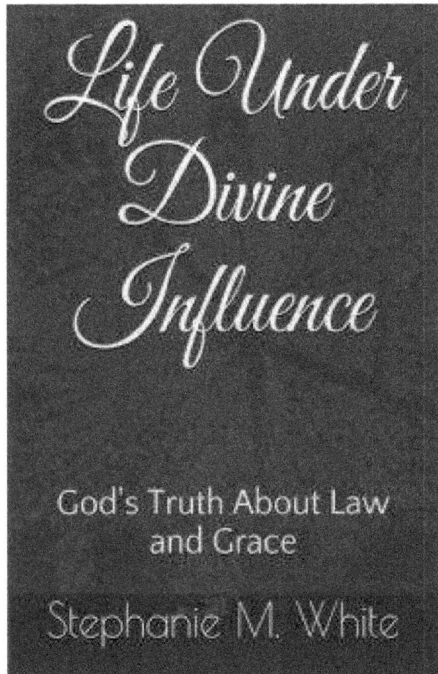

The Christian life is not meant to be complicated.
Jesus Christ came to give us an abundant life, a life full of
Spiritual fruit, a life of freedom and victory.
Unfortunately, religion has infiltrated our lives and it has
robbed us of this gift. We were not created to earn or achieve
from God but we were created to receive from Him and display
His love and goodness in our lives. We were created to live
under His Divine influence and we were created to walk in His
Spirit.
As we begin to learn more about God's plan for our lives, we will
begin to experience the good life God planned for us to live - a
life under His Divine influence.

https://whitestephanie83.wixsite.com/heavenonearthforyou

More books by Stephanie White

Heaven on Earth: it is a life most people believe is not possible to achieve, but according to God's Word that is exactly what we can have! Heaven on Earth takes you on a journey through the Word of God so that you can find out what is available to you as God's child and you will also discover how to enjoy this life to the fullest.

Everyone experiences an off-season in life - sometimes more than one. An off-season is a dry time; it is a time of lack and a time of trials. These times can feel daunting and painful; therefore, we must understand the purpose of these times and we must be sure that God has a plan for our good and His glory.

As Christians, we must understand that we have two natures - our Spiritual nature and our flesh. Each nature wants to dominate, but only one can. This book will take you through a thorough study of your two natures and it will help you understand each one. It will also show you how to rule over your flesh and defeat its power in your life.

https://whitestephanie83.wixsite.com/heavenonearthforyou

WORDS OF LIFE DEVOTIONALS
by Stephanie White and Kathleen Higham:

Available now!

SUMMER EDITION   FALL EDITION   WINTER EDITION

Each daily devotional is a ninety-day journey
through the Word of God.

COMING SOON

https://whitestephanie83.wixsite.com/heavenonearthforyou

A SEASON OF GRIEF
is a unique devotional designed to facilitate those who have suffered loss and are grieving.

Grief can bring even the strongest to their knees. As we endure a season of grief we will experience a myriad of emotions that we cannot ignore. As you read through this devotional you will find encouragement to deal with these feelings and move forward in spite of them because you are abiding in the Word of God.

We must invite Christ into our season of grief; we must take in His Word and receive the healing that only He can provide.

Our loved ones who have gone on ahead of us want us to enjoy the life that we have left; they want us to remember them and smile and look forward to being reunited with them.

The Word of God is our life. It is meant to be our daily life. This devotional will help you incorporate the Word of God into your life even as you press past the pain of loss.

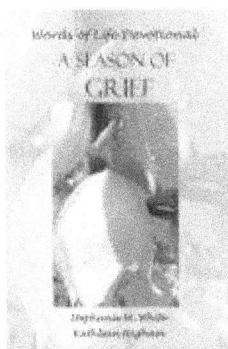

WORDS OF LIFE DEVOTIONAL ~ A SEASON OF GRIEF EDITION

https://whitestephanie83.wixsite.com/heavenonearthforyou

https://whitestephanie83.wixsite.com/heavenonearthforyou

INTRODUCTION

As we journey through this life as a Christian we repeatedly find ourselves in discouraging situations. I believe as Christians we need to understand the purpose of these challenging times and we must discover God's plan for them. In the book of first Peter we find that trials have a purpose.

1 Peter 1:6-9 (NIV)   In this you greatly rejoice, though now for a little while you may have had to suffer grief in all kinds of trials.   These have come so that your faith--of greater worth than gold, which perishes even though refined by fire--may be proved genuine and may result in praise, glory and honor when Jesus Christ is revealed.   Though you have not seen Him, you love Him; and even though you do not see Him now, you believe in Him and are filled with an inexpressible and glorious joy, for you are receiving the goal of your faith, the salvation of your souls.

The testing that we undergo establishes the validity of our faith. Genuine, Spiritual faith is the result of consistently abiding in the Word of God – it comes from taking the Word of God in repeatedly. True faith is a fruit of the Word.

As we continue on this journey of life our faith is essential. Eternal value is assigned to our faith; therefore, we must study it and understand what it is, how we obtain it, how it works, what classifies it as genuine, what its benefits are, and so on. As you commence on your journey into this realm of faith you may need to adjust your thinking. What you discover about faith may surprise you and it may challenge what you have been taught and what you have been influenced to believe. Allow God's Word to be your point of reference and open your eyes to the truth of the Word. In John chapter eight, verse thirty-two, Jesus tells us that only through abiding in the Word do we discover the truth; in so doing, we become personally acquainted with the Word and sequentially we are set free. I am trusting that you will find the freedom you have longed for in this book, freedom that can only come through abiding in the truth of God's Word.

Chapter 1
FAITH DEFINED

Hebrews 11:1 (KJV)
Now faith is the substance
of things hoped for, the evidence of things not seen.

A proper definition of faith is necessary if we are going to completely understand faith. God's Word defines faith as *the confidence we have with regard to what we are eagerly anticipating.* Faith is our guarantee of the unseen.

Faith is the substance (or assurance) of things "hoped" for – hope is defined as earnest expectation. A person who lives in expectation can be compared to a child eagerly anticipating Christmas. The child waits with an energized expectancy that persists even when Christmas does not arrive as quickly as they would like. They will even encourage others as to the certain arrival of Christmas. Living in expectation produces a good attitude; it produces joy, peace, and enthusiasm about life. A person who lives in expectation is a joy to be around. They are not depressed and downtrodden; they are optimistic as they look forward to the fulfillment of God's Word.

When someone mentions the word "hope" we may mistakenly assume that they are wishful rather than certain. "Hope" has been used interchangeably with the word "wish" and because of this we may find ourselves misunderstanding the Word of God. **Biblical hope is defined as expectant anticipation; it has nothing to do with wishing.** Chance has nothing to do with the hope that the Bible speaks of. Faith does not need physical proof. Faith only requires the Word of God.

Faith, we can conclude, is the *guarantee* of what we are expecting; however, that surety is blind. Faith is not based on something that we can see; on the contrary, it is based on the unseen. Faith does not need physical proof.

Romans 4:18 (NIV) Against all hope, Abraham in hope believed and so became the father of many nations, just as it had been said to him, "So shall your offspring be."

Genuine faith believes against all hope or against what the circumstances would make one expect. It believes when there is absolutely no natural reason to believe.

Faith is not based on you, your circumstances, your "good deeds," or others; genuine faith is exclusively founded on the Word of God.

Many times the Word proclaims promises which, in the natural, have no earthly reason to be expected. I would even go so far as to say that *most* times those things which we are promised in the Word lack proof in our *natural* circumstances. In the same way Abraham had to believe against all hope, we will have to do likewise. Abraham was old in age as was his wife; they were lacking any evidence that would imply they should have a child. In fact, all of their circumstances demonstrated the complete opposite of the promise that God had made to them.

As we begin to live in the Word of God we will uncover promises that appear to be as likely as the moon being composed of cheese; however, appearances can be deceiving. The Word even boldly announces that appearances *are* deceiving and we are not to be betrayed by them (John 7:24, 1 Samuel 16:7). As a Christian, we are not bound by what we see.

2 Corinthians 5:7 (KJV) For we walk by faith, not by sight.

The definition of faith entitles us to believe without any physical corroboration.

2 Corinthians 4:18 (NIV) So we fix our eyes not on what is seen, but on what is unseen. For what is seen is temporary, but what is unseen is eternal.

The Word of God makes clearly proclaims that we are not limited by what we see physically. If truth be told, we will have to disregard many of the things we see if we are going to live by faith. In order for us to live by faith we must become skilled at fixing our eyes on the unseen; staying focused on the Word will be our main objective. The Word informs us of how things *should be*; it also produces the faith we need to believe these things *will be*. The sole source of faith is the Word of God. It is fundamental that we are in agreement with the fact that we cannot acquire faith without the Word of God.

Romans 10:17 (NIV) Consequently, faith comes from hearing the message, and the message is heard through the word of Christ.

You will have to remain focused on the Word of God, as opposed to your circumstances, if you are going to live by faith. Fixing your eyes on the unseen requires a *steady* diet of the Word of God.

Faith, at times, has been misunderstood due to the improper use of the Word of God. In the same way that you can misuse a chair by standing on it or sitting only on two legs, we can misuse the Word. People have faith in a chair's ability to hold them because of their experience with the chair. If every time you sat in a chair it would collapse under your weight, you would then soon lose your faith in the chair. A sturdy chair will not just collapse under a person; the person must cause the collapse by using the chair in a way it was not designed to be used. People have progressively lost faith in the Word because of improper use. Many times we use the Word as a rulebook instead of a love letter; this misuse hinders faith. Instead of reading to be in relationship with our Savior, we are reading because we falsely believe that it will keep us in His good graces. This is undeniably wrong. The Word is for *our* good; it is *our* tool to stay away from sin and to walk in the Spirit.

The Word is not something we must try to live up to; the Word is the *way* to live! The Word was designed to enable us to live a Spiritual life – not for us to attempt to conquer it in our flesh.

We must use the Word correctly. We must see the Word of God as the love letter that it is and we must abide in it. If we are misusing the Word and it is not coming to pass in our lives, then we only have ourselves to blame in the same way the chair is not to blame when we misuse it.

Faith comes from a Spiritual source which is the Word of God; therefore, faith is eternal the same as anything Spiritual is, in fact, eternal.

Psalms 119:89 (NIV) Your Word, O LORD, is eternal; it stands firm in the heavens.

The Word is eternal; faith is eternal.   We must understand that faith can never be depleted. As long as you are alive you have the opportunity to walk by faith and see God bring His Word to pass in your life!

Ecclesiastes 9:4 (NIV) Anyone who is among the living has hope--even a live dog is better off than a dead lion!

Hope is trust and confidence – it is a byproduct of faith or a byproduct of the Word in your life. If you are reading this, then you have hope!   Do not let Satan deceive you into believing that you have gone too far, you have done too much, or you have passed the point of no return. We have a living hope; the Word of God is our proof that we *can* see change. We have the privilege of going to the Word for everything we need.

If I desire change in any area of my life, then I need to discover what God's Word says on that subject. My consistent intake of the Word will produce faith and that faith will produce Spiritual actions in me; whatever needs carried out in my life can *only* be accomplished through the Word!

As we define faith it is important that we define "works of faith" as well. Faith is the result of hearing the Word of God, taking it in, and making it part of who you are; therefore, a work of faith is an action that is the outcome of the ingested Word being worked out of you. There are two kinds of works: those done by faith and those done by the flesh.

James 2:18 (ESV) But someone will say, "You have faith and I have works." Show me your faith apart from your works, and I will show you my faith by my works.

James 2:26 (ESV)   For as the body apart from the spirit is dead, so also faith apart from works is dead.

Faith, which is produced by a steady intake of the Word, will produce Spiritual actions in your life. Works or actions *can* be accomplished apart from faith; however, those actions are classified as dead, meaning *of the flesh*. If your faith does not produce a Spiritual action in your life, then it is dead. Dead faith is *not* Spiritual; it is *not* the result of living in the Word of God. Dead faith is a belief based on the flesh and any actions associated with it will also be of the flesh. Living faith is produced courtesy of the Word of God and it is the only way to produce Spiritual fruit in your life. Instead of focusing on what *we* are doing, we must focus on the Word of God and allow the Word to do the work in us!

> **Matthew 17:20 (Ampl.) He said to them, Because of the littleness of your faith [that is, your lack of firmly relying trust]. For truly I say to you, if you have FAITH [THAT IS LIVING] like a grain of mustard seed, you can say to this mountain, "Move from here to yonder place, and it will move; and nothing will be impossible to you."**

The word "littleness" is not found in the original translation; only the word "unbelief" is found. Size is not of the essence here – life is. Only living faith, or Spiritual faith, will produce the actions we long for. Equating faith to a mustard seed demonstrates the life-giving power of faith and its potential to do the impossible in your life. The mustard seed is one of the smallest seeds but it becomes one of the largest garden plants (Mark 4:31-32) and a provisional source.

Your faith may seem inconsequential; but make no mistake, it is most important in your life. Its significance is found in its source – the living Word of God.

Faith does not need to be spoken for; faith speaks for itself in the form of actions. Faith, which comes from abiding in the Word, will produce Spiritual actions in us over time. Living, Spiritual faith will produce Spiritual fruit; it is impossible for faith to remain fruitless. The Word of God, speaking of itself, tells us that it will not come back void; it will produce fruit (Isaiah 55:11). It is impossible for us to abide in the Word and not see Spiritual fruit eventually produced in our lives. We can prove our faith, or the time spent in the Word, *by* our Spiritual fruit. We do not have to tell everyone how Spiritual we are, how much faith we have, or how much time we spend in the Word; it will be evident by our behavior, our words, and our attitudes as we continue to abide.

It is all too often that we *think* we believe, yet our lives are screaming out that the opposite is in fact true! If I say that I believe God is in control of my finances, yet I worry about paying my bills, I complain about high prices, and I am stingy with the money I do have, then I do not possess living, Spiritual faith in regards to my finances. My actions declare loud and clear what I truly believe. The person who pays their bills peacefully, retains joy no matter what the prices are, and possesses the ability to give – that person has living, Spiritual faith pertaining to their financial situation.

It is important for us to notice the difference between the works of the flesh and the works of the Spirit. Another important distinction is the longevity of each. The works of the flesh will not last, but those done by faith will. Works of the flesh see their reward, if there is any, here on earth and their reward goes no further. The works of the Spirit, however, are of eternal significance. When you are abiding in the Word of God it is active in you and it is being worked out of you (or it is being accomplished in your life); and accordingly, works of eternal value are being produced, works that are the end result of taking in the Word of God.

1 Thessalonians 1:3 (NIV) We continually remember before our God and Father *your work produced by faith*, your labor prompted by love, and your endurance inspired by hope in our Lord Jesus Christ.

Work, spiritual work, is exclusively produced by faith and faith works by love (Galatians 5:6). It is critical that we ingest this truth; otherwise, we continue on with the misconception that we produce Spiritual works on our own via our love, fear, discipline, or some other counterfeit vehicle. There is absolutely no other method for producing Spiritual works.

John 3:6 (NIV) Flesh gives birth to flesh, but the Spirit gives birth to spirit.

Works of the flesh come from the flesh in the same way works of the Spirit come from the Spirit. It is impossible for our flesh to produce any Spiritual work in the same way it is impossible for our Spirit to produce any work of the flesh.

The Word is Spirit and the Word produces faith and faith produces Spiritual works.

John 6:63 (NIV) The Spirit gives life; the flesh counts for nothing. The words I have spoken to you are spirit and they are life.

As we abide in the Word of God we will become increasingly aware of transformations in our behavior, our words, our thoughts, and our motives. The more we are in the Word the more we will take note of these changes. The work faith does in our lives is a process; your actions will not change overnight.   The Word produces faith – faith that will progressively produce Spiritual actions. Faith sets us free, free from attempting to produce "Spiritual" actions on our own. *We* no longer have to force ourselves to be "good!" What a relief! Works of faith come effortlessly, not by struggle or human effort; works of the Spirit are a work of God. God does the work in us *as* we focus on Him (the Word). Works of the

Spirit or works of faith are invaluable; in fact, any other work is of *no* value in the kingdom of God.

> **1 Corinthians 3:11-13 (NIV) For no one can lay any foundation other than the one already laid, which is Jesus Christ. If any man builds on this foundation using gold, silver, costly stones, wood, hay or straw, his work will be shown for what it is, because the Day will bring it to light. It will be revealed with fire, and the fire will test the quality of each man's work.**

The foundation has been laid and it is Jesus Christ and Jesus Christ is the Word of God (Revelation 19:13). As I live my life as a Christian it is my prerogative to ignore the Word of God, but if I choose to do this, I must understand the consequences.

> **Psalms 127:1 (NIV) Unless the LORD builds the house, its builders labor in vain. Unless the LORD watches over the city, the watchmen stand guard in vain.**

Any work that we do on our own, or in the flesh, is of no value; we are building in vain. Understanding this is of utmost value to the Christian; it is the key to having purpose.

The Bible tells us that the "quality" of our work will be tested – quality denotes the source or the origination. Simply put, this means that everything we do here on earth will be tried by fire and this trial by fire will expose the origination of the work. The quality, or origination, of our work will be tested. Any work that does not originate from the Word is worthless.

What would be the source or the origination of your works? Do your works originate from your flesh or the Word of God? Are you doing what you do by human effort or are your works those that come naturally in view of the fact that you abide in the Word of God? Ask yourself why you do what you do. One day I was taking my grocery cart back to the cart return and I asked myself why I was doing it. I began to think about a message I heard that encouraged you to return your cart. I knew I needed a verse from the Word of God to be the source of my action. God brought "Do unto others as you would have them do to you," to mind. I smiled. I was reminded of what Jesus said about doing for others; His Word was my seed.

Satan has deceived Christians for long enough; it is time for us to be sensitive to the fact that apart from Christ we cannot produce Spiritual fruit (John 15:5). We no longer have to vainly attempt to work for something that Christ has already provided for us.

In our discussion of works it is important for us to call attention to the truth that our salvation is not based on our works. Salvation is founded on our acceptance of Jesus Christ and His sacrifice for our sin. Far too often, Christians doubt their salvation because confusion begins to make them question. They begin by simply believing salvation is through Christ alone; nonetheless, as time progresses, they find themselves believing that they need to live by their own strength and perform to a certain Spiritual standard. When they cannot succeed, they then begin to doubt their salvation. We can put an end to the doubt by committing verses such as John 15:5, John 3:6, and John 6:63 to heart. No one can produce Spiritual fruit outside of Christ.

Romans 7:18 (Ampl.) For I know that nothing good dwells within me, that is, in my flesh. I can will what is right, but I cannot perform it. [I have the intention and urge to do what is right, but no power to carry it out.]

There are two parts to every Christians. We have our Spiritual identity and we have our flesh. The flesh may want to do what is right, or what is Spiritual, but it cannot. Our flesh cannot produce Spiritual fruit; Christ in us is our *only* hope of glory. If we desire holiness, then we must abide in Him; He *is* holy and when we are found *in Him* that is when we are holy.

If we desire Spiritual works, then we must abide in the Spirit; in other words, we must live in the Word of God. The Word of God empowers us!

My works will be judged based on their source. If the foundation of my action was my flesh I will not receive a reward; a reward is only bestowed for a Spiritual action and a Spiritual action always has a Spiritual source. Faith (which originates from the Word) is the source of all Spiritual actions and those actions are the only ones that will be rewarded.

In light of the fact that these actions are Spiritual, we can, without doubt, discern that true possession of these rewards is not rightfully ours. These actions that "we" have produced were only the result of Christ in us and the Word working through us. Without the Spiritual source the Spiritual action would have never been possible. Is it any wonder that we will lay our crowns at *His* feet?

We have clearly identified that faith is a Spiritual fruit, with a Spiritual root, from a Spiritual Seed. Faith is only produced through the Word of God and we can only apply the Word of God in our lives if Christ lives in us. Faith is an essential part of our lives; we are told to live by it! As we begin our study of faith we will find that it is the Spiritual Seed that we require if we want to generate Spiritual fruit, if we want to avoid sin, if we want to please God and if we want to see God's promises come to pass in our lives. It is safe to say that faith is essential for the Christian! When God instructed us to live by faith He was in essence directing us to live in His blessings! Living by faith is living a life that is producing Spiritual fruit, living a life where you are steering clear of sin, living a life that is pleasing to God and living a life where you are basking in all of His promises! No one can imagine a life more superior than that. As someone I know once said, "It is a life of *Heaven on Earth*!"

Chapter 2
HOW FAITH WORKS

Galatians 5:6 (KJV)
For in Jesus Christ neither circumcision availeth any thing, nor uncircumcision; but faith which worketh by love.

We have defined faith and now we are going to investigate how faith works. God's Word tells us that faith works by love. Faith is made active or effective by love; love makes faith active and effective. Faith is displayed by love. Love must be the foundation on which faith operates. As mentioned, most of God's promises tend to be opposed to what we see in the natural; in order for us to believe that these pledges from the Word of God are intended for us, we *must* be living in the love of God. Only true love freely gives and bestows undeserved gifts. If I believe God's love for me is limited, then I will also believe that there are restrictions on His promises that He made to me. **Unconditional love is the foundation of faith.**

Faith works by love; in other words, faith is made active by love or faith is shown by love. Without love faith will not work; it will not be effective.

1 Corinthians 13:13 (NIV) And now these three remain: faith, hope and love. But the greatest of these is love.

Faith, hope, and love remain or endure, and they always will, but the greatest of these is love. Greatest entails the largest or the loudest; it also means the elder. It is preeminent; it is unsurpassed. Without love you would not have faith or hope. Since love is the greatest we should find out what love is.

1 John 4:10 (NIV) This is love: not that we loved God, but that He loved us and sent His Son as an atoning sacrifice for our sins.

Love is God sending Jesus to die in our place. Jesus Christ came to earth to die for me because I could not pay the price for my sin without going to a place called hell and being eternally separated from Him. Hell is a place prepared for the devil and his angels; it was not prepared for man (Matthew 25:41). It was never God's plan for man to spend eternity separated from Him; God's plan is for man to accept His Son's sacrifice (2 Peter 3:9). What interrupted God's plan? In short, Adam and Eve doubted God in the garden. This doubt initiated the entrance of sin into the world and all became sinners; nonetheless, through Christ all have the opportunity to become righteous (Romans 5:17). Christ displayed the Father's love for us in the ultimate way: He gave His life for ours. Man now has a choice; man has to decide to receive or reject the sacrifice Christ made for him – and not receiving is rejecting. When we receive Christ's sacrifice for us, something transpires – love is made complete in us. Love becomes the basis for our lives – His love for us becomes our foundation on which we build.

With His love as our foundation we can then begin to build with faith.

2 John 1:6 (NIV) And this is love: that we walk in obedience to His commands. As you have heard from the beginning, His command is that you walk in love.

This verse, and others like it, has confused too many Christians for too many years.

When we believe that our love for Christ is proven by the number of commands we do not break, we are sadly mistaken. Love *enables* us to walk after His commands; without Christ we cannot avoid sin.

Love is the foundation that faith works by and *faith* is the architect of the Spiritual fruit in our lives – we are not. "Walking in obedience" means to walk after, to walk at large, or to walk as a companion. Love is a relationship and we walk as Christ's companion *through the Word.*

Walking in Spiritual obedience is not some effort or attempt to be perfect on our part; it is the end result of our focus and daily attention to the Word.

It is important for us to understand that the Word is not a rulebook; it is His love letter to us. As we begin to see the Word as His love letter to us, rather than a rulebook, a change takes place. Love changes us; loves changes everything. Faith works by love and faith produces Spiritual actions instead of the flesh-centered actions. We must understand that faith, not anything in and of ourselves, produces Spiritual fruit or actions in our lives.

James 2:26 (NIV) As the body without the spirit is dead, so faith without deeds is dead.

Faith without deeds is dead. What does that mean? In Christ we are alive; in our flesh we are dead. Any deed that we produce in our flesh is dead; any deed that we produce in our Spirit is alive. We can have faith that is alive or faith that is dead. We can believe something based on our Spirit or we can believe something based on our flesh. When we believe something in our Spirit it is what I call "living faith;" subsequently, when we believe something in our flesh we can classify it as "dead faith." We must understand that even though we are saved we still have to deal with our flesh. If we assume that we can somehow love God enough to do good works on our own, then we are walking in the flesh and we are only producing dead deeds – no matter how Spiritual they may *appear*. A person can go to church, donate money, be married, raise children, or help others, and do it all for naught simply because they did not accomplish any of it by faith. The Word of God was missing from their life and as a result they were merely creating deeds of the flesh.

Appearances can be deceiving, bear in mind, and *we* can be deceived even by *our own* appearances! Our deeds are only Spiritual when they come from the Spiritual source. Do not be deceived by the specious facade of your actions. Test your actions; take the time to discover how you do what you do!

Faith works or is activated by love; faith is shown by love. Love is God and God is the Word or the source of faith. Without the Word you do not have faith and without faith you do not have Spiritual actions. We can ignore the fact that without the Word of God we will never produce Spiritual fruit, but doing so only hurts us. The Word of God is the Source for anything and everything Spiritual we desire!

We have looked at what love is, seeing that faith works by love, but let us also look at some of the many facets of love; this will help us better understand faith as well.

1 Corinthians 13:4-8 (NIV) Love is patient, love is kind. It does not envy, it does not boast, it is not proud. It is not rude, it is not self-seeking, it is not easily angered, it keeps no record of wrongs. Love does not delight in evil but rejoices with the truth. It always protects, always trusts, always hopes, always perseveres. Love never fails. But where there are prophecies, they will cease; where there are tongues, they will be stilled; where there is knowledge, it will pass away.

Love is patient; and since faith is activated by love, faith will demonstrate patience. We will base an entire subsequent chapter on patience; because of this, we will move ahead to the fact that love is kind for now. Love is kind; as a result, faith demonstrates kindness. When your faith is Spiritual you will likewise express kindness.

Psalms 145:17 (ESV) The LORD is righteous in all His ways and kind in all His works.

Kindness, like any Spiritual fruit, is produced by abiding in the Word of God. Kindness is a quality that God possesses. Our kindness is proof that our faith is Spiritual and not a derivative of our flesh. If we believe based on our flesh, then it will not be possible to be kind. For example, if you struggle financially and someone asks to borrow money, then your reaction can help you appreciate what kind of faith you have. If you react in a *genuinely* kind manner, then your faith is Spiritual; if you react in an unkind way or think in an unkind way, then your faith is of the flesh. Your reactions can help you determine what kind of faith you possess. Bear in mind that this is simply a gauge for you to discover where you are – it is not intended to invoke guilt. If your faith is not Spiritual, then you can know that you need more of the Word – you do not need to berate yourself.

Another facet of love is a lack of covetousness. Love does not envy; for that reason, faith does not envy. We will not live envious of others who have received God's promises if we are walking by faith. Why would we? If we truly believe God, then we are truly expecting to receive; an envious person is jealous simply for the fact that they do *not* expect to obtain that very thing that someone else has.

James 4:2 (NIV) You want something but don't get it. You kill and covet, but you cannot have what you

want. You quarrel and fight. You do not have, because you do not ask God.

The person who wants but does not receive is also envious. A lack of receiving is credited to a lack of asking. "Asking" comes from a Greek word that means to call for or to require. Asking is not a timid request; definite knowledge precedes Biblical asking. Receiving will never be the result of human effort; it will always be the result of faith. The Word of God is your absolute proof; it provides you with the confidence you need to ask for what you desire while providing you with happiness for those who already possess the very thing you are waiting for.

1 Chronicles 17:25 (NIV) You, my God, have revealed to Your servant that You will build a house for him. So Your servant has found courage to pray to You.

David's confidence was the result of what God had communicated to him. Our confidence is fostered likewise. God has communicated to us through His Word and His Word reveals all of the awesome promises that God has in store for us. As we discover these promises and abide in them, confidence is cultivated in our lives. It is established to the point that we go to God for what He has promised and we go boldly!

If someone I know receives a healing and I look forward to receiving a healing, then I have no reason to be jealous of their healing. I am only envious when I believe I will never receive what they have. One sure way to test yourself to know if you are in faith or in the flesh is to give yourself the "jealousy test." If you assume that you believe God in the area of finances, then consider someone you know who is extremely blessed financially and be honest with yourself regarding how you feel about them and their blessing. If you find that you are jealous, you must then recognize that your flesh is at work and you must quickly decide to employ the Spirit of God that resides in you. Go to God for the help that you need! Look up verses that relate to jealousy and begin to meditate on them; remain focused on the Word. Only the Word will produce the Spiritual change that you need in your life.

We also find that love does not boast and it is not proud. Love is not proud nor does it boast and neither does faith because **faith is a result of the Word of God; it is not the result of any human effort.**

Ephesians 2:8-9 (KJV) For by grace are ye saved through faith; and that not of yourselves: it is the gift of God: not of works, lest any man should boast.

Romans 3:27-28 (NIV) Where, then, is boasting? It is excluded. On what principle? On that of observing the law? No, but on that of faith. For we maintain that a man is justified by faith apart from observing the law.

Living, Spiritual faith is void of boasting and pride due to the fact that we cannot take any of the credit when we are walking in the Spirit. Being in agreement with God puts us in a place of humility. If we produce any Spiritual fruit, then it is only thanks to God and we are exceedingly aware of this! A person who boasts about what they do for God, the amount they do for God, the things they refrain from in regards to sin, and so on, is clearly not living by faith since faith works by love and love does not boast.

What is your position in regards to boasting? Do you take credit for the things *you* do? We must be honest with ourselves in regards to where we are; acknowledging the problem is the starting point for your victory over it. If we are in the habit of taking credit for the "Spiritual" things we *think* we do, then we need to make some changes. These changes will only take place as we focus on the Word – specifically the Word on humility.

It is of the essence that we put an end to pride; pride paves the way for our fall. It is also imperative for us to understand that this sense of pride we undergo is a *false* sense of pride in view of the fact that we are unable to accomplish anything Spiritual apart from Christ.

Love is also the opposite of rude; it is polite. Faith will likewise exhibit politeness. The Bible tells us that we are to live by faith; it is to be our lifestyle. If this is the case, then we will also live a lifestyle of courtesy. Are we polite? Do unbelievers have manners that supersede ours? Do waiters or waitresses walk away from our table delighted that we were their customers? Do we treat them with respect? Are we courteous to clerks at the stores and others in public places or are we rude?

Faith behaves graciously. If we are walking by faith, then we are living a life based on the Word of God; we are living a life of expectancy. We believe that God will perform the awesome things that He has promised in His Word and that hopeful expectancy puts us in an advantageous frame of mind. The Bible tells us that as we think so we become – when our mind is right our actions follow. Rudeness is the result of a damaged mental condition; but be of good cheer, the condition of our mind can be repaired by the Word of God.

We also find that love is not self-seeking, it is not easily angered, and it keeps no record of wrongs. Love displays forgiveness and forgetfulness; faith likewise exhibits the actions of forgiving and forgetting.

Ephesians 4:32 (NIV) Be kind and compassionate to one another, forgiving each other, just as in Christ God forgave you.

Faith and love are Spiritual and forgiveness is Spiritual. To reiterate, anything Spiritual has only one Source – the Word of God (and the Word is God, John 1:1). Faith is the result of the Word and faith produces forgiveness in us.

Forgiveness will not be impossible when we are abiding in the Word. The Word reveals to us that God has forgiven us; once we receive that forgiveness, we can then forgive others. We can only give what we have received – that is why Jesus told us it was better to give than to receive. The person who can give has received!

We cannot give what we have not first received – if we have not accepted Christ's forgiveness, it will then be impossible for us to forgive others. The power to forgive is a gift from God that we must receive.

As we abide in the Word it becomes part of who we are; we take on the characteristics of the Word. We no longer have to force ourselves to forgive others; forgiveness (and every other Spiritual fruit) will come naturally, by faith.

In our study of love we also find that love rejoices with truth; for that reason, faith rejoices with truth. Faith is a fruit of the Word and the Word is truth; therefore, faith is truth.

John 17:17 (NIV) Sanctify them by the truth; Your Word is truth.

The Word is truth; if we want to walk in truth, then we must abide in the Word.

Faith shows forth truth. It displays God's Word or His promises. Our lives should reflect the vows that He has made to us in His Word – and they will, *as* we live by faith. The Word of God tells us that we will be living memorials that declare God's faithfulness to His promises (Psalm 92:15). Our lives will display His goodness and His faithfulness.

Another characteristic of love is protection. Love protects and equally does faith. Faith is a protection mechanism for the child of God.

Ephesians 6:16 (NIV) In addition to all this, take up the shield of faith, with which you can extinguish all the flaming arrows of the evil one.

Faith is our shield; it is our protection. Faith was defined as something we believe based on the Word of God even when we have no visible proof. Faith is the Word of God alive and at work inside of us and it protects us from our flesh and the devil! The Word of God will keep us safe from every one of his traps. Faith defeats the enemy every single time because faith is the result of the Word; faith is our victory!

We are also protected by faith because faith produces Spiritual fruit in our lives. Spiritual fruit protects us from the flesh.

We must view all of God's Word as His promises – if you find a verse that instructs you in regards to your behavior, then that is a promise, too! If you walk in the Spirit, then you will not yield to the flesh –sin will not have dominion over you if you are abiding in the Word of God.

As we continue on with the many facets of love we find that it always trusts, hopes, and perseveres. Love, as well as faith, is trustworthy. Faith comes from the Word of God and the Word is something we can trust. We do not have to speculate about the verity of the Word. We do not have to question whether or not God will keep His promises.

Faith displays hope; it is full of expectancy. A person who lives by faith is perpetually anticipating more from God. They are content: satisfied, but not settling. The person who lives by faith also persists in what they say they believe. They do not give up when their faith gets tested. Faith shows forth perseverance. Genuine faith outlasts any test! Genuine faith, the same as unadulterated love, never fails!

Now that we have looked at an abbreviated description of love and its assorted facets, I trust that this aids in your understanding of how faith works and how faith displays itself in your life. Keep in mind that faith works by love; it is made active or effective by love, it is shown forth by love. As you fill yourself with God's love letter, God's love for you makes faith active in your life and that faith is displayed to others through the many facets of love.

Love must be your foundation. We can only build on Jesus Christ and what He has done for us; therefore, we must keep ourselves immersed in His love.

Jude 1:21 (Ampl.) Guard and keep yourselves in the love of God; expect and patiently wait for the mercy of our Lord Jesus Christ (the Messiah)-- [which will bring you] unto life eternal.

We guard ourselves by remaining in His love; the love of God is our protection. When we are abiding in His love we will be safe from fear, condemnation, jealousy, and the like.

Surround yourself with the love of God; keep yourself at the center of His love and enjoy the work that faith does in your life! Faith will provide you with everything you need to wait on God's timing for your victory.

Chapter 3
THE ORIGIN OF FAITH

Romans 10:17 (NIV)
Consequently, faith comes from hearing the message, and the message is heard through the word of Christ.

Faith, just like everything else, has an origin; we have found that faith's origin is the Word of God. Too many Christians are trying to manufacture faith outside of the Word. In the same way that you cannot produce a carrot without a carrot seed, you cannot produce faith without the Word; the Word is the Seed. Faith is not something we decide to possess. I have heard myself make the statement, "I am just going to believe God;" unfortunately, at the time, I did not realize how erroneous that statement was. I cannot make a decision to believe. **Living, Spiritual faith is a *result*; it is *not* a *decision*. It is the outcome of abiding in the Word of God.**

How many Christians are fooled into believing that they possess faith when they, in reality, do not?

2 Corinthians 13:5 (ESV) Examine yourselves, to see whether you are in the faith. Test yourselves. Or

do you not realize this about yourselves, that Jesus Christ is in you?--unless indeed you fail to meet the test!

You can test yourself and prove if you have Spiritual faith by asking yourself one simple question, "What verses do I have to back up what I say I believe?" If you cannot provide verses that support what you say you believe, then you do not have Spiritual faith. You need the Word if you desire Spiritual faith; Spiritual faith will move the mountains in your life!

Luke 8:9- (NIV) His disciples asked Him what this parable meant. He said...This is the meaning of the parable: The seed is the Word of God. Those along the path are the ones who hear, and then the devil comes and takes away the word from their hearts, so that they may not believe and be saved. Those on the rock are the ones who receive the word with joy when they hear it, but they have no root. They believe for a while, but in the time of testing they fall away. The seed that fell among thorns stands for those who hear, but as they go on their way they are choked by life's worries, riches and pleasures, and they do not mature. But the seed on good soil stands for those with a noble and good heart, who hear the word, retain it, and by persevering produce a crop.

No one lights a lamp and hides it in a jar or puts it under a bed. Instead, he puts it on a stand, so that those who come in can see the light. For there is nothing hidden that will not be disclosed, and nothing concealed that will not be known or brought out into the open. Therefore consider carefully how you listen. Whoever has will be given more; whoever does not have, even what he thinks he has will be taken from him."

As we study faith we study the parable of the seed. **The seed is the Word of God.** We must clearly understand this truth. All too often, Christians are planting everything *but* the true seed. A popular phrase in Christianity is, "If you have a need, plant a seed;" however, Christians are confused as to what the seed truly is. If you have a financial need planting a "seed" of money is a popular misconception; nonetheless, the seed that needs to be planted is the seed of the Word of God. If you have a financial need, then you must *first and foremost* find as many verses as you can on the promises God has for your financial needs and you must meditate on them. As you abide in these promises faith will grow and that faith *will* produce Spiritual actions. Giving will become a natural occurrence in your life *because of* the faith you have developed in regards to your finances. When you give simply because you have a need and you give without faith, you are giving in vain. It is giving done in the flesh, void of faith, and anything that is without faith is sin (Romans 14:23). We must plant the seed of the Word and that seed will produce faith *as well as* Spiritual actions.

The Spiritual actions are also part of the *blessing* of the Word; do not be confused and imagine that the actions are what inherit the promises. The promises come to pass in your life *as a result* of faith and patience (Hebrews 6:12) *alone*; the Spiritual actions, as well as faith, are the result of abiding in the Word – *you* did not produce either!

Now that we understand what the seed is we can move on to the various types of ground. We see four types listed: the path, the rocks, the thorns, and the good ground. We will first study the path. The seed that fell along the path represents people who "hear" but do not retain what they hear. Why does this happen?

Matthew 13:19 (ESV) When anyone hears the word of the kingdom and does not understand it, the evil one comes and snatches away what has been sown in his heart. This is what was sown along the path.

Understanding is the key to retention. What then is understanding? The word "understand" comes from a Greek word that means to be united with or together by association and companionship. Understanding has to do with your union with Christ. Your association with Him is what procures the retention of the Word. To understand, therefore, means you recognize who you are in Christ and you walk in that identity. I was discussing the meaning of the word "understand" with my dad one day and he summed it up like this, "When you understand you "stand under" the umbrella of who you are in Christ." I liked that!

When we speak of understanding in reference to our relationship with the Word it means to read as a companion of Christ. In Christianity, far too many born-again children of God are reading as outsiders. They do not understand who they are in Christ and because of this the Word of God becomes nothing more than a rulebook to them. They feel condemned and criticized as a result of the time they spend in the Word as opposed to feeling energized, equipped, and encouraged. Why would anyone want to spend time in the Word when they are walking away with such negative results?

If we are not reading the Word in a Spiritual manner, in lieu of our new identity, then we are wasting our time. The time we spend in the Word must be a Spiritual action! If we do not "understand" what we read, then it is only being taken from us; it is not producing faith in us. Satan is a thief, but if a strong man guards his possessions the thief does not have a chance (Luke 11:21)! We can guard what is ours by recognizing who we are in Christ. Faith works by love and we must be acquainted with His love for us. If we do not identify with how much He loves us, then we will find it next to impossible to believe the promises in His Word. His love is an attractive force that will draw us to His Word thus producing the faith we require.

> **Proverbs 15:14 (Ampl.) The mind of him who has understanding seeks knowledge and inquires after it and craves it...**

The person who looks at the Word as a rulebook is not seeking to read and spend time in the Word; they look at the Word as their duty. The person who knows who they are in Christ, in contrast, longs to read; they are seeking answers and Spiritual faith from the Word. They literally crave the Word and they are excited about spending time in it. The Word is their ally, not their enemy! They retain the Word because of the amount of time they spend in the Word and the relationship they have with it.

The next type of ground was rocky ground. The seed that fell on the rocky ground was lacking moisture; Jesus described this seed as "having no root." This seed had the ability to produce but only for a *limited* time. Without roots the seed lacked anchorage. The roots provide stability, food, and moisture; without them, the life of the seed is fleeting. The seed on the rocky ground is received with joy but that is where it ends. Too many times the Word is received with emotion. Excitement only lasts for so long; our emotions cannot be allowed to control us seeing that they are subject to change. We can easily be excited by the Word but that excitement can even more easily fade away. If we are not rooted in the Word of God, then we too will experience a short-lived (if any) harvest.

John 8:31-32 (NIV) To the Jews who had believed him, Jesus said, "If you hold to My teaching, you are really My disciples. Then you will know the truth, and the truth will set you free."

Jesus advised the Jews who believed in Him that there was a distinction between believing in Him and being His disciple; He is advising us as well. A disciple is a student, a student of the Word or the teachings of Christ, and they *hold* to the Word. They *abide* in it. We can be a born-again Christian, but not a disciple. A disciple has roots; his roots are in the Word of God. He clings to the Word and he continually abides in it. This type of Christian is the one who walks in true freedom.

As we will study in detail in a subsequent chapter, our faith will be tested. Without roots, the testing will pluck us out of the ground! Believing is easy when that which we believe for is not challenged; having your faith tested requires depth! Notice "as the seed grew," and "they believe for a while;" both denote a period of time. You can believe uncontested for a period of time, but eventually your faith *will* be tested.

1 Peter 4:12 (KJV) Beloved, think it not strange concerning the fiery trial which is to try you, as though some strange thing happened unto you.

Trouble and persecution will come because of the Word you are hearing; your faith will be tested. The trial is not some strange occurrence that you cannot explain; it is something God already foretold. The children of Israel were also told about something. God prophesied that He would provide bread for them in the wilderness; yet, when it arrived they called it "manna." Manna can be defined by one question, "What is it?" They considered the provision strange in the same way we look at the trial as being strange. Why? God has already informed us that it will come; faith *will* be tested. When the test comes your way do not say, "What is this?" Instead, say, "I was waiting for you and I am ready for you!" What they called manna was bread; God calls our enemies bread as well (Numbers 14:9). These trials are bread for us! If we treat these trials in a Biblical manner, then we will take in more of the Word as a result of these trials. We will look at the trial as bread and we will eat; as a result, the more we are in the Word the more roots we develop.

If you do not develop roots you will wither away! No roots equals no endurance when the trouble and persecution come. Roots are evidence of time. An interesting fact about a tree is that the longest branch is only as long as the longest root; what you see above ground is the outcome of what you do not see below ground. As we mature in Christ we "grow roots." We must continue in the Word and be rooted and grounded in Christ! Others cannot see the Word of God that you store up in your heart, but they will not be able to ignore the effects of that Word in your life! Jesus told us that what is hidden will be revealed (Luke 8:17); the Word of God that is being hid in your heart will be revealed in your life!

The third type of ground is thorny soil. The thorny soil is a metaphor for the cares and luxuries of this world. Either one can take our focus off of Christ. Paul said he knew how to be abased *and* how to abound. He knew how to deal with lack and he knew how to handle abundance; we must learn how to do the same. The instruction we require is found in the Word of God. Lack can lead us to works of the flesh in the same way wealth can if we are not focused on Christ. A person can be generous in the flesh as easily as they can be greedy. Too many times we are deceived by the "supposedly" Spiritual action based on appearance.

Regardless of the act is that is being accomplished, if faith is not the origin of that action, then it was done for nothing; it is sin.

This seed on the thorny soil is described as being "choked" by cares, riches, and pleasures. The seed of the Word can very easily be drowned out by cares, riches, or pleasures if we are not mature. The Christian who is focused on Christ can handle the problems that come their way as well as the blessings! Riches in the hands of a mature Christian are an amazingly awesome tool. Churches are built, the hungry are fed, the homeless are housed, orphanages are constructed and manned, debts are paid for those who would otherwise be incapable, and the list goes on. In the same way, problems in the hand of a mature Christian become a testimony to the awesomeness of God and His desire to be our Provider, Deliverer, and so much more!

Cares, riches, and pleasures are only "thorny ground" as long as we are focusing on our flesh. If we allow these things to take our focus off of the Word, then we are void of the very thing that facilitates our ability to handle each of these. God designed things to be pleasurable for us, but we can become addicted to those things and spend more time with them than with God; and in that case, those pleasures are choking the Word. Video games, computers, and the wide-range of entertainment that we have readily available to us daily are contending for our time. These things in and of themselves are not wrong; they can be used in the wrong way, however, and become thorny ground. If the things you are devoting your time to are choking the Word in your life, then you need to reevaluate your priorities.

Finally, we come to the good ground. This ground describes the Christian who knows who they are in Christ and who continually abides in the Word of God. The Word is the origin of faith. Faith comes from hearing the Word and faith is provided courtesy of the Word. The Word will produce faith in us and it will bring about everything God has promised us in His perfect timing. Fruit is brought forth with patience; instantaneous results are not the norm. A farmer does not sow a seed and immediately expect a harvest; he waits for the seed to grow and produce. He waits in expectation knowing that what he has planted *will* generate a crop. For weeks he has no visible proof that anything is happening. In the same way that we have no visible proof that God's promises to us will come to pass many times, the farmer must also go by faith. Good ground will accept the seed and nurture it.

At the end of this parable of the seed we find that whatever is hidden will eventually be revealed. Continue to bear in mind that the seed that is hidden under the ground does eventually manifest and the seed of the Word that you are hiding inside of your heart will become apparent as well! Do not feel discouraged despite the number of times you quote the same Scriptures, regardless of how habitually you read the same verses, and in spite of how many times you pray the same promises. What you do in secret between you and God concerning faith will be manifested and one day it will be revealed and come to light! We now understand that no one may be acquainted with all of the hours that you are focusing on the Word and praying for your child or your marriage or your finances or whatever your problem may be; but when your breakthrough comes, when God's promises are revealed in your life, they will not be able to miss it! The seed that is planted will sprout; the fruit will be noticeable. We cannot see the seed, just like we cannot see the roots of a tree, but we sure can see the longest branch – we can see the result!

We are told to "take care then how you hear." *How* are you hearing the Word?

James 1:25 (KJV) But whoso looketh into the perfect law of liberty, and continueth [therein], he being not a forgetful hearer, but a doer of the work, this man shall be blessed in his deed.

Take care how you hear. Do not become a "forgetful hearer" – looking and continuing produce "the doer." The forgetful hearer is the casual listener. He may hear the Word but he does not take it in and make it part of who he is; he does not continue in the Word. Continuing in the Word will enable us to produce Spiritual actions because continuing in the Word produces faith.

How are you hearing the Word? What kind of soil are you? Do you lack an understanding of who you are in Christ and consequently read the Word as an outsider? Do you turn your time with the Word into a duty instead of a privilege? Are you the rocky soil? Do you lack the roots that you need to make it through the testing of your faith? Are you the thorny ground? Do you allow lack, excess, or entertainment to choke the Word in your life? The good soil is what we were all created to be! We have been given a new heart, a heart that is attentive to the Word, a heart that is longing to take the Word in; it is our choice to employ that new heart.

Be aware of what kind of ground you are. If you are taking the Word in, retaining it, and continuing to do so, then expect more – Jesus told us we would be given more and more seed. The person who typically ignores the Word will lose the little he *thinks* he has. Do not be misled concerning the seed you have. Good ground receives the seed and produces. Are you producing? Is the Word producing attitudes, actions, thoughts, feelings, and so forth, which agree with the Word in your life? If we are not producing, then we can be sure that we are not hearing in the correct way!

We must understand the value of the Word in our lives. It is described in Deuteronomy as our life (Deuteronomy 32:47). The Word is our foundation for everything Spiritual!

Mark 4:13 (Ampl.) And He said to them, Do you not discern and understand this parable? How then is it possible for you to discern and understand all the parables?

Jesus told us that this parable regarding the Seed is the key to understanding all parables. If we do not understand the Word and what it is to us, then we will be lost as Christians. The Word of God is our Source for everything Spiritual we require! It is of the essence that we understand what blocks the Word in our lives and what allows the Word to thrive. We must grasp the fact that the Word is our Seed for all Spiritual fruit; it is the *one* thing we necessitate.

We are told that the Word is what provides us with entrance into the Promised Land and it is what enables us to remain there. The Promised Land is a place where we are at rest in Christ; we are totally dependent on Him for everything. In the Promised Land God is clearly the Provider; He is completely depended upon. Christians find themselves in the wilderness when they depend on what they think they can do outside of the Word.

We must be absolutely certain of the origin of faith. We desperately need to understand the value of the Word in our lives. As we recognize the origin of faith we will progressively live in the Word more; as a result, faith will produce all of its awesome fruit in our lives!

Chapter 4
IN ADDITION TO FAITH

2 Peter 1:3-7 (NIV)

His divine power has given us everything we need for life and godliness through our knowledge of Him who called us by His own glory and goodness. Through these He has given us His very great and precious promises, so that through them you may participate in the divine nature and escape the corruption in the world caused by evil desires. For this very reason, make every effort to add to your faith goodness; and to goodness, knowledge; and to knowledge, self-control; and to self-control, perseverance; and to perseverance, godliness; and to godliness, brotherly kindness; and to brotherly kindness, love.

In first Peter we are told to "add" attributes to our faith. The way in which this is phrased can easily lead us to believe that this is something we must attempt to do on our own; in fact, it even states to "make every *effort*." The original language the Bible was written in clearly indicates something contrary. "Make every effort" comes from the original phrase, "giving all diligence," which means to bear in alongside or introduce simultaneously with speed or haste. The word "add" comes from the Greek word, *epichorēgeō*, which means to furnish besides, that is, fully supply, aid or contribute, and to minister nourishment. We have learned thus far that faith comes from hearing the Word of God; faith is produced in our lives as we abide in the Word. We have also discovered that faith produces Spiritual actions in our lives; faith produces Spiritual works.

The production of faith that is accomplished by the Word of God will simultaneously produce or bear in alongside these Spiritual attributes: goodness, knowledge, self-control, perseverance, godliness, brotherly kindness, and love. *Faith*, because of its source, supplies us with or furnishes these Spiritual qualities or attributes.

Faith is Spiritual in the same way these attributes are Spiritual and nothing that is Spiritual can be produced without the Spiritual source of the Word of God. The Word will produce faith and along with faith it will furnish us with the qualities listed. It is *His* divine power that has given us everything we need for life and godliness; it is nothing that we can achieve somehow on our own. Through His own glory and goodness we receive the Word of God (or His very great and precious promises) and the Word is the only means whereby we can take part in the Divine nature and break away from our flesh. It is by the Spirit that we overcome the flesh.

Romans 8:13 (NIV) by the Spirit you put to death the misdeeds of the body…

It cannot be reiterated enough that we cannot accomplish Spiritual actions or fruit apart from Christ. We necessitate the Word of God! It is not an option.

We cannot "add" Spiritual attributes to our lives without the Word of God. The Word produces faith and faith produces the attributes; faith that is alive will produce Spiritual actions in me.

When we defined faith we looked at James, chapter two verses eighteen and twenty-six, and we found that faith will produce an action unless it is dead or unspiritual. If your life is not displaying Spiritual actions, then it is only because you do not have Spiritual faith at work in your life.

2 Peter 1:8-9 (NIV) For if you possess these qualities in increasing measure, they will keep you from being

ineffective and unproductive in your knowledge of our Lord Jesus Christ. But if anyone does not have them, he is nearsighted and blind, and has forgotten that he has been cleansed from his past sins.

Possession of Spiritual qualities is the result of using the Word of God or the knowledge that we have been given.

Through the Word I become effective and productive in my Christian life; the Word enables me to produce Spiritual fruit and take on my Spiritual identity while leaving my flesh behind.

Ignoring the Word will do the opposite. Our lack of the Word will keep us from possessing the Spiritual qualities faith provides us with. Three reasons for ignoring the Word are listed in the above verse: we are too focused on ourselves, we look at the Word as a rulebook instead of a love letter, and we forget what Christ has done for us. No matter what our reason for overlooking the Word, the results are the same: no Word equals no faith and no faith equals no Spiritual fruit or actions. We will remain in sin without the Word.

Psalms 119:11 (KJV) Thy Word have I hid in mine heart, that I might not sin...

Faith keeps us out of sin; it does so because of its root: the Word of God. The Word produces faith and the Word keeps us out of sin. The more Word we store up inside of our hearts the more faith we produce, the more Spiritual fruit we display, and the less sin we are involved in.

This verse in Psalms ends with "against Thee" in most translations, but those two words are not found in the original text. We are not sinning against God; we are hurting ourselves. God tells us that He gave us His Word so that it would go well *with us*, not Him. When we find ourselves in our flesh then we must go to the Word; we must go to Christ. If we feel like we are doing something "against" Him, then we may feel that we need to stay away from Him.

Sin is misunderstood many times. Phrases such as "willful sin," "perpetual sin," and "living in sin," just to name a few, have confused many. These phrases are used to explain away certain verses, but what people fail to realize is that we are *all* perpetually living in sin. No one is exempt from daily sin. Worrying, thinking wrong thoughts, fear, gluttony, and laziness are just a few daily sins that people are "living" in – and many times they are doing so "willfully." Why are these sins overlooked when others are spotlighted?

2 Corinthians 10:12 (NIV) We do not dare to classify or compare ourselves with some who commend themselves. When they measure

themselves by themselves and compare themselves with themselves, they are not wise.

We spotlight certain sins because we compare them with other ones. We must refrain from categorizing; our own sin always seems excusable, but it is still in fact sin. We look at murder and lying as two different things rather than recognizing both as sin – sin that nailed Jesus Christ to the cross.

James 2:10 (NIV) For whoever keeps the whole law and yet stumbles at just one point is guilty of breaking all of it.

If all you ever did was tell a lie, then God says you are still guilty of breaking every single law! That includes murder, rape, adultery, and so on. It is not wise for us to categorize sin; doing so can give us a false sense of superiority.

Too many Christians deem themselves esteemed in God's eyes (and man's) because they are not involved in certain sins and that is wrong. Any honor we possess is only thanks to Jesus Christ. It is only through Him that we can avoid and refrain from sin.

If you have never been physically involved in a particular sin you should not pat yourself on the back; you should bow down and praise God!

2 Corinthians 1:12 (NIV) Now this is our boast: Our conscience testifies that we have conducted ourselves in the world, and especially in our relations with you, in the holiness and sincerity that are from God. We have done so not according to worldly wisdom but according to God's grace.

Holiness and sincerity, along with *every* Spiritual fruit, are *from God*. Worldly wisdom, or our flesh, cannot produce any Spiritual fruit. We will only see these things come to pass in our lives by the grace of God. Understand that the grace of God is His divine influence on our hearts and our lives; this influence comes into our lives through the Word of God. You will only see Spiritual fruit as the result of the Spiritual seed of the Word of God; therefore, our boast is in the Word or Jesus Christ (1 Corinthians 1:31; Jeremiah 9:23)! Our boasting is in vain when we are bragging on ourselves. In our flesh no good thing dwells. Our flesh is void of the ability to produce Spiritual fruit.

1 John 3:9 (KJV) Whosoever is born of God doth not commit sin; for His seed remaineth in him: and he cannot sin, because he is born of God.

Because this verse (and others like it) is not rightly divided it is often misunderstood; therefore, various explanations are necessary. The explanations, though deemed necessary by man, are incorrect. We are told to study the Word in order to be able to rightly divide the Word – to know what is of the Spirit and what is of the flesh. In this verse in first John we see that whosoever is born of God does not sin; rightly dividing this will eliminate the confusion.

Who is born of God? The Spiritual part of a man is born of God – not the flesh. Our Spirit does not sin; it *cannot* sin. If we do not rightly divide this verse, then we will have to explain it away with phrases like "continual sin" or "willful sin." I have heard this verse taught and continual or willful sin was used as the scapegoat for the truth. It does not say that whoever is born of God will not live in continual, willful sin; yet, many will explain this verse just that way. They may even do so haughtily supposing that they are not involved in continual or willful sin. They may deem themselves worthy of the title of "one who does not sin."

Truly, we must see ourselves the way God sees us. *In the Spirit* we are seen as "one who does not sin;" it is not because we are not occupied with what *we* consider continual or willful sin.

"Willful sin" is simply a bogus explanation for verses like the one in first John. What does the Word of God have to say about "willful" sin?

Psalms 19:12-13 (NIV) Who can discern his errors? Forgive my hidden faults. Keep Your servant also from willful sins; may they not rule over me. Then will I be blameless, innocent of great transgression.

Willful sin is the same as hidden sin as far as God is concerned. Sin is sin to Him; it is the result of your flesh, period. Why then do we categorize? Sin is sin and the entirety of it can only be conquered through Christ! He must keep us from sin and He does so through the Word.

He has given us His Word as our weapon to fight sin and He has given us His Spirit that is incapable of sinning. If we utilize the Word we have been given, we are then walking in His Spirit and we are denying the flesh its desire to sin.

The Word of God is our key to *everything* we need for life and godliness. Through the Word we can attain everything we need to reign in this life in a godly manner. Too many times Christianity separates this life from godliness when Jesus Christ combines the two. The Word of God gives us everything we need for both! When we abide in the Word we are provided with *everything* we need.

We were created with a body, a soul, and a Spirit. Our Creator designed us this way and our Creator is also our Sustainer; He did not create what He did not plan to maintain. He cares about every aspect of our lives. If we believe that He is only interested in the "Spiritual" matters that we are involved in, then we are limiting His access in our daily lives.

We must also realize that as a Christian we can make anything we do Spiritual. For example, cleaning the house can be a Spiritual activity when we do it through Christ. We do not have to separate the every-day from the Spiritual. God cares about *all* that we are involved in. He says that the very hairs of our head are numbered (Luke 12:7), He tells us that He wants to bless *everything* we put our hands to (Deuteronomy 15:10), and He mentions by name plenty of the day-to-day needs that He wants to supply.

It is our choice to accept or refuse His daily provision. The Israelites refused. We also refuse when we do not agree with His promises. Even though the Word clearly proclaims the blessings that God has for us, there are many Christians who believe they are not supposed to be blessed. If we do not agree with the Word in regards to the blessings, then we will not receive them.

Do not make the mistake of believing that you must *add* to your faith; instead, open your eyes to all that faith *includes*!

1 Samuel 9:24 (Ampl.) And the cook lifted high the shoulder and what was on it [indicating that it was the priest's honored portion] and set it before Saul. [Samuel] said, See what was reserved for you. Eat, for until the hour appointed it was kept for you, ever since I invited the people. So Saul ate that day with Samuel.

We need to see what is reserved for us! This Spiritual vision is the result of the Word. If we are lazy with the Word, then we will not know what God has for us and we will give up what is rightfully ours!

1 Samuel 9:20 (Ampl.) As for your donkeys that were lost three days ago, do not be thinking about them, for they arc found. AND FOR WHOM ARE ALL THE DESIRABLE THINGS OF ISRAEL? ARE THEY NOT FOR YOU AND FOR ALL YOUR FATHER'S HOUSE?

The Kingdom of God is full of desirable things and they are all for us and our families! *We* need to see them. We must keep our eyes on the Word in order for us to see what rightfully belongs to us. In many locker rooms the ultimate prize the team is contending for is posted for all to see. The coach wants them to be reminded daily of what they are fighting for. Before they ever play their first game they are thinking about being the last team standing at the end of the season. It is important for us to do the same. What are you reminding yourself of daily? Do you see the ultimate prize ahead of you or are you too focused on the trial you are dealing with?

After we see what is ours we then must abide in it! We must prepare for the fight for our faith. These promises are for the "hour appointed," or as stated in Habakkuk chapter two, "the appointed time," or "the end fulfillment." We must wait for them; we must endure the trial until it has completed its work. Experiencing God's promises requires faith *and* patience and we can only wait as a result of the Word – the Word produces the faith and patience in us that are called for!

Do not miss out on what is yours; you are meant to receive from God! You are meant to enjoy all that God has for you. Recognize what faith includes and begin to live in it. Realize you will have to fight for your faith at times. Do not let the fight intimidate you; this fight is a good fight and God provides you with everything you need to fight it. Prepare now! Discover what God has for you and abide in those promises; abide until the appointed time –*know* that there *is* an appointed time. His Word *will* come to pass. Faith *is* worth fighting for!

Chapter 5
FAITH IS A FIGHT

1 Timothy 6:12 (NIV)
Fight the good fight of the faith.
Take hold of the eternal life to which you were called
when you made your good confession in the presence
of many witnesses.

Faith; it is amazing. We have defined it and we have found that, next to love, it is unequivocally the most important Spiritual fruit. Faith is produced by the Word (Romans 10:17); it is what pleases God (Hebrews 11:6); it is the only source we possess that enables us to produce Spiritual actions in our lives (James 2:18); it keeps us away from sin (Psalms 119:11); it brings God's promises to pass in our lives (Hebrews 6:12). It is essential to point out that love is the greatest but we also know that faith works, or is to be active, by love; therefore, faith and love work in concert. To claim faith's importance is in no way devaluing love's preeminence.

In defining faith we established that **faith is the result of the time we spend in the Word of God**. It is imperative that we reestablish the fact that faith is not a virtue we simply decide to possess. I cannot make a decision to believe God and thus enter into faith; faith is not acquired in this manner. Faith can *only* be obtained through hearing the Word of God. Abiding in the Word produces faith *naturally* in my life; **faith will not be attained as the result of any human efforts.**

Faith can be a fight; but do not be dismayed, it is a *good* fight! In the above mentioned verse, Paul is writing to Timothy and he informs him that he must fight in order to take hold of the eternal life to which he was called, but in saying this he is careful to point out that this fight is a good one.

Paul defines faith as a fight so let us define the word "fight."

> FIGHT: a place of assembly (as if led), a contest (held there), conflict, contention, race.

The noun "fight" is defined as a contest or a place of assembly that someone is led to. I find the "as if led" aspect of this definition quite fascinating; this denotes that we do not necessarily usher ourselves into this fight. There are times that *God* leads us into a fight for our faith.

> **Deuteronomy 8:2 (ESV) And you shall remember the whole way that the LORD your God has led you these forty years in the wilderness, that He might humble you, testing you to know what was in your**

heart, whether you would keep His commandments or not.

God will lead us into a fight for our faith at times. A humbling situation attests to what we are made of. If we have been storing the Word in our heart, then the situation will not catch us off guard and we will "keep His commandments." To keep His commandments denotes keeping our focus on the Word of God and keeping it hedged in our lives. The word "keep" was translated from the Hebrew word *shamar*. To *shamar* the Word is to remain focused on it, to protect it in your life, to hedge it in, and to attend to it.

Too many times we reject the Word of God during times of struggles. Too often we incorrectly conclude that keeping His commandments refers to never "breaking" any of the mandates.

A person who "keeps His commandments" is a person that is vigilant with the Word of God; they abide in it, they focus on it, and they protect it in their lives.

The test to know what is in our heart is for us, not for God. He already knows what is in our heart; He is opening our eyes to what is truly stored up in our hearts because, interestingly enough, we deceive ourselves many times.

As we continue on with our dissection of the fight of faith we also need to define the word that was translated as the *verb* "fight."

> FIGHT: to struggle, to compete for a prize, to contend with an adversary, to endeavor to accomplish something.

We need to fight the fight. We need to contend with an adversary at the place of testing we are led to. Our flesh is the adversary – and it will fight for control. Jesus is familiar with fighting this fight and He is our example.

> **Luke 4:1-4 (NIV)   Jesus, full of the Holy Spirit, returned from the Jordan and was led by the Spirit in the desert, where for forty days He was tempted by the devil. He ate nothing during those days, and at the end of them He was hungry. The devil said to Him, "If you are the Son of God, tell this stone to become bread."   Jesus answered, "It is written: 'Man does not live on bread alone.'"**

Jesus was led to a destination by the Spirit; this place was a desert. God will direct every one of His children to a location where they will contend; there will be times when we will have to fight for what we assume we believe. When what we allegedly believe is put to the test will we pass or will we have to take the test again? Jesus passed; He passed with the Word. When Satan approached Him, Jesus fought back with the Word of God; we should follow His lead. For instance, if the wrong thoughts are attacking your mind, then you must promptly focus on Scripture. An attempt to think happy thoughts or beating yourself up for not having your thought life under control will be of no profit. **You will find it is impossible to triumph over the enemy without the Word of God.**

Romans 8:2 (Ampl.) For the law of the Spirit of life [which is] in Christ Jesus [the law of our new being] has freed me from the law of sin and of death.

The law of the Spirit of life is the prescription for life as God has it and it is *only* found in Christ. We must abide in the Word; the Word is Spirit and the Word is life. As we abide in the Word, we of necessity must comprehend who we are in Christ. In doing this we are set free from the law of sin and death; we find ourselves liberated from our flesh. The flesh no longer controls us but, through the Word, we control our flesh!

Romans 12:21 (NIV) Do not be overcome by evil, but overcome evil with good.

Overcoming evil can only be accomplished with good; God is good and God is the Word (Mark 10:18, John 1:1). In order for us to "fight the fight" we must be prepared spiritually. Spiritual preparation entails Scriptural understanding and retention. Storing up the Word of God in our hearts will enable us to fight this good fight. The Word of God is essential; it is the source of your faith and it is the sustainer of your faith.

Hebrews 12:2 (NKJV) Looking unto Jesus, the author and finisher of our faith...

The fight for your faith cannot be fought without the Word / Jesus. Without the Word you cannot have faith, and the Word is what consummates faith. Once again, it must have the Spiritual source; it is impossible to draw attention to this too much!

Fighting the good fight of faith will not always resemble a walk in the park. As we delve further into the temptation of Christ we will take note of His situation. He was tempted for forty days by the devil and for the duration of this time He did not consume food; most of us experience pain from missing *one* meal. Imagine being tempted for forty days *excluding* the fasting aspect! The temptation in and of itself is strenuous enough; the addition of a body that has been deficient of nourishment for forty days only heightens the experience.

Christ's temptation is usually taught as a three-part temptation; however, when we read Mark and Luke's accounts carefully they inform us that the three recorded temptations were the *final* temptations. We are not aware of the actual number of temptations He underwent during those forty days; the Bible never enumerates, it only states that He was in fact tempted for forty consecutive days. The Bible also tells us that He was tempted in *every* way.

Hebrews 4:15 (NIV) For we do not have a high priest who is unable to sympathize with our weaknesses, but we have one who has been tempted in every way, just as we are--yet was without sin.

In the same way Satan attacked Jesus in the areas he concluded Jesus would be vulnerable, he will do the same with us. He tempted Jesus with turning stones into bread knowing that Jesus had fasted for forty days; however, he underestimated the satisfaction the Word of God provides to the hungry.

The Word of God will fill our every need if we only give it the occasion; abide in the Word and experience its riches.

Man does not live by bread alone, but by every word of God. It may not always be easy to live by the Word, but it will always be worth it; faith *is* a good fight.

The fight of faith is defined in the original language as a struggle, a competition, and a contention. It is also defined as an endeavor to accomplish something. In this fight we must keep in mind the "something we are endeavoring to accomplish," lest we allow the struggle to get the best of us. We know that Jesus endured the cross even though He despised the shame because of the joy that was set before Him (Hebrews 12:2); if we are going to endure our trials, then we must keep the things that we desire to accomplish set before us. Paul told Timothy to fight the good fight of faith with the purpose of taking hold of the eternal life to which he was called as his motivation. If we are going to endeavor in successfully taking hold of eternal life, then we must establish what eternal life is.

Eternal life was translated from the word *Zoë*. *Zoë* is a word that defines life as God has it. *Zoë* was the life that was present in the Garden of Eden. *Zoë* is the life that God originally intended for mankind to possess but sin destroyed that life. Sin entered the garden as the outcome of a lack of faith.

Genesis 3:1 (NIV) Now the serpent was more crafty than any of the wild animals the LORD God had

made. He said to the woman, "Did God really say, 'You must not eat from any tree in the garden?'"

"Did God really say?" Your faith is the prize that Satan is contending for and it has been since man's creation. As long as Satan can cause you to doubt, he has you exactly where he wants you. Doubt is sin.

Romans 14:23 (NIV)   *...everything* that does not come from faith is sin.

Faith comes from the Word; consequently, anything and everything that is not the result of the Word *is* sin. No matter how you package your actions, if they are not a product of the Word of God, then they are sin! Satan does not care if you give money at church; he only cares if you doubt God's Word concerning your finances *as* you give. Satan is not bothered by the care you give your children; he is only interested with whether or not you believe what God promised you concerning them *as* you care for them. Satan does not mind if you abstain from cheating on your spouse; he only wants to make sure that you look at another and lust after them in your mind and heart *as* you "refrain" from physically being with another. I can go on but I trust you understand the illustrations.

Christianity is not a matter of appearances; it is a matter of faith.

In the book of Revelation (chapter three, verses fifteen and sixteen) we find that Christ does not want us to be lukewarm. What is lukewarm? Lukewarm is a combination of hot and cold; in Spiritual terms it is a person who tries to accomplish the Spiritual through their flesh. We can do what *appears* Spiritual but if our action was accomplished by the flesh Jesus is not going to receive it; He will spit it out.

Eternal life is the goal we desire to accomplish in this fight for our faith. Bear in mind that eternal life is *Zoë* or life as God has it, and do not confuse eternal life with eternity in heaven. Many times the Scripture names eternal life when it is not referring to your habitation in heaven. Eternal life can be referring to living a life on earth *now* as it is in heaven and that is the present goal we desire to accomplish. We know that this objective will be a fight; nonetheless, we must press on recognizing the benefits of this fight. Remind yourself to keep your goal set before you in order for you to possess the strength to continue on even in the tough times.

Proverbs 29:18 (KJV) Where there is no vision, the people perish: but he that keepeth the law, happy is he.

A vision is a mental sight. We must keep our goal before us or keep it in sight and as we do this we will experience happiness. Keeping the law makes us happy. Again, to most people the phrase "keeping the law" denotes achieving perfection in regards to rules, but this is not the case. Do not ignore the fact that the word "keep" was translated from a word that means to keep your eyes on. **The person who keeps their eyes on the Word of God is happy.** The person who keeps the Word of God in front of them, or before them, is happy; they are blessed! They have a mental sight, one that is based on the Word of God. In their mind's eye they can see what God has planned for them; they look forward to it with excited anticipation; they keep the joy set before them.

In this fight for our faith, we must keep the Word of God as our focus if we want to thrive. The people perish where there is no vision; death is the end result for the person who does not keep their eyes on the Word. Death is living a life in the flesh or living a life outside of the Spirit; it is living a life that is the opposite of the *Zoë* life. *Zoë* life will only be accomplished as we abide in the Word of God.

Zoë life is a gift from God; but just like any gift, it must be received. We receive the gift of life through the Word of God. The Word produces the faith we necessitate to live out what Christ died for us to have.

Romans 6:17-23 (NIV) But thanks be to God that, though you used to be slaves to sin, you wholeheartedly obeyed the form of teaching to which you were entrusted. You have been set free from sin and have become slaves to righteousness. I put this in human terms because you are weak in your natural selves. Just as you used to offer the parts of your body in slavery to impurity and to ever-increasing wickedness, so now offer them in slavery to righteousness leading to holiness. When you were slaves to sin, you were free from the control of righteousness. What benefit did you reap at that time from the things you are now ashamed of? Those things result in death! But now that you have been set free from sin and have become slaves to God, the benefit you reap leads to holiness, and the result is eternal life. For the wages of sin is death, but the gift of God is eternal life in Christ Jesus our Lord.

Wholeheartedly obeying the form of teaching that we are entrusted with refers to hearing the Word and producing faith. Again, we must not ignore the original translation. The original word for "obey" is the Hebrew word *shama*. To *shama* the Word means to listen intently or to hear intelligently. Faith comes from hearing. As we abide in the

Word, the faith that we require will flourish in our lives and we will understand who we are in Christ. The Word will produce the faith necessary to release us from sin and free us to live a righteous life in Christ. We will not offer ourselves to the flesh when we *shama* the Word. To offer means to yield or stand beside. I must continue to yield to righteousness or stand beside Christ – He is my righteousness.

Yielding to righteousness is nothing more than yielding to, or focusing on, the Word of God in order for us to live out who we are as a Christian: Christ-like. We are offering ourselves to righteousness; this is accepting who we are in Christ and living accordingly. In doing this, we refrain from sin; we are set free from the things that produce death (the fruits of the flesh) in our lives. The wages of sin is death. The compensation you receive from sin is a life in the flesh but, praise God, eternal life is His gift to us! We can enjoy life as God has it when we live by faith.

Are you willing to fight for what is rightfully yours in Christ or are you a person who gives up when things get tough?

Nehemiah 4:14 (NIV) After I looked things over, I stood up and said to the nobles, the officials and the rest of the people, "Don't be afraid of them. Remember the Lord, who is great and awesome, and fight for your brothers, your sons and your daughters, your wives and your homes."

Fear will prevent us from fighting for our faith. Fear is the opposite of faith; it is the result of forgetting what God has said. In Nehemiah he encourages them to remember God; he reminds them that there is no reason to fear *provided* they remember God. He does so after he "looks things over." Many times we truly do not look at our situation according to the Word of God. When you are faced with a situation you need to look it over in comparison with the Word. If it does not line up with the Word, you must then look at what the Word has to say about changing your situation.

God can do the impossible; He can turn your situation around! Bringing God into remembrance will endow us with the courage we require to fight for our homes and our families. Stand up! Speak the Word! When you do, fear will not be able to stop you!

Does this fight sound too aggressive for you? Would you rather sit back and not fight?

Numbers 21:4 (Ampl.) And they journeyed from Mount Hor by the way to the Red Sea, to go around the land of Edom, and the people became impatient (depressed, much discouraged), because [of the trials] of the way.

The children of Israel had so much ahead of them. God's promises to them were substantial. Even with the

Promised Land ahead of them they grew weary. Along the way they encountered trials that tested what they believed. Would they believe God's promises or their circumstances? Our trials are prolific in nature but what they produce does not have to be something negative. The fight for our faith does not have to leave us "impatient, depressed, and much discouraged;" we have the ability to press on with Christ. He can lead us through with patience, joy, and encouragement. If you are going through a fight for your faith and you feel impatient, depressed, and discouraged, do not feel down about yourself. That will not accomplish anything. To overcome the impatience, depression, and discouragement, we must employ the Word of God; we must abide in His presence (Psalm 16:11).

The trials are inevitable, but depression is not! We do not have to give in to the problems.

> **Isaiah 50:10 (Ampl.) Who is among you who [reverently] fears the Lord, who obeys the voice of His Servant, yet who walks in darkness and deep trouble and has no shining splendor [in his heart]? Let him rely on, trust in, and be confident in the name of the Lord, and let him lean upon and be supported by his God.**

We must understand that the fight for our faith does not signify that our focus is not on Christ. We can be abiding in the Word and still endure a time of trials. The trial is there to make us stronger; it is not designed to undermine our Spiritual identity.

As a child of God we have the right to peace and joy, but that right is not always called for by the Christian. Call for joy; call for peace. Summon the Spiritual in your life. It is rightfully yours in Christ; you do not have to live without it. God is inviting you to lean upon Him and be supported by Him. What will you do with His invitation?

To be deficient in joy, a good life, and the ability to "shine," is pointless seeing that you were created to display His splendor!

Isaiah 49:3 (NIV) He said to me, "You are My servant, Israel, in whom I will display My splendor."

God wants to display His splendor in us; splendor is originally translated as glory in the King James Version. His servant is the one in whom He will be glorified.

GLORIFIED: A primitive root; to *gleam*, that is, (causatively) *embellish*; figuratively to *boast*; also to *explain* (that is, make clear) oneself; to *shake* a tree: - beautify, boast self, go over the boughs, glorify (self), glory, vaunt self.

God wants to explain who He is to others through *your* life. What does a life of defeat and depression express to others? The words "boast" and to "vaunt self" articulate to us that He does not want to communicate anything less than His best through us! This splendor will be displayed in us as we rely on the Lord and become confident in Him. Reliance and confidence are a derivative of the time we spend in the Word of God. The more of the Word we have in us, the more we can correctly demonstrate who God really is.

In order for God to demonstrate Who He is through our lives we must rely on Him, trust in Him, have confidence in His name and be supported by Him. Unfortunately, many Christians must endure a trial before they find themselves doing just that. Part of the definition of "glorified" is to shake a tree. I find this interesting. When a tree goes through a storm it is shaken; consequently, anything that is dead is blown off of the tree. At the end of this ordeal the tree finds itself in a better state as a result of the storm. You may feel shaken by the fight you are going through for your faith, but keep in mind the end result. There are times when the dead things need to be removed in order for the real beauty to have a chance to display itself. The more of the flesh that is removed the more of Christ's Spirit that is revealed!

The fight for our faith does not have to leave us "splendor-less!" In fact, it is meant to do the opposite. We can shine as bright as the Son when we abide in Him regardless of the circumstances!

Fight for your faith. Do not allow the flesh to win. Abide in the Word, focus on Christ, and let His love flow through you and give you the victory!

Do not misunderstand me, I realize we will have our moments. We will have our days when we cry and feel like giving up, but the anchor of the Word will ultimately bring us back to our firm foundation. The more time we spend in His presence the more joy we will experience. When you begin to feel the depression or the impatience or the discouragement closing in you, must immediately fight back with the Word. Do not give your flesh time to linger and take root!

In this fight, you must understand your role. Do not take on a role that is not yours to take.

2 Chronicles 20:17-18 (Ampl.) You shall not need to fight in this battle; take your positions, stand still, and see the deliverance of the Lord [Who is] with you, O Judah and Jerusalem. Fear not nor be dismayed. Tomorrow go out against them, for the Lord is with you. And Jehoshaphat bowed his head with his face to the ground, and all Judah and the inhabitants of Jerusalem fell down before the Lord, worshiping Him.

In this fight I will take up my position of praise and worship; I will stand firm in my faith by abiding in the Word thus seeing the deliverance God promises to give me in His Word. Fear will be removed through faith (faith that comes from abiding in the Word); discouragement will disappear through the encouragement of the Word. I can face the day; I can face the trial because God is with me. I will bow my face to the ground – I will humble myself seeing that apart from Christ I can do nothing and I will continue to live my everyday life through Him! I will not allow the fight to defeat me; I *will* obtain the victory through Christ!

Faith may be a fight, but it is a good one. Never forget the outcome of your faith!

Keep your focus on the Word of God and be the "tough" one in this battle! A boxer will train for several months for a fight that lasts minutes; train yourself! The stronger the contender, the easier the battle. The stronger you become, the weaker the flesh becomes in your life. Train yourself with the Word of God and be strong. Victory is yours in Christ – even though it takes time and even if it never seems like it will happen for you!

Chapter 6
A ROUND LOST

Judges 20:17-21 (NIV)
Israel, apart from Benjamin,
mustered four hundred thousand swordsmen, all of
them fighting men. The Israelites went up to Bethel
and inquired of God. They said, "Who of us shall go first
to fight against the Benjamites?" The LORD replied,
"Judah shall go first." The next morning the Israelites
got up and pitched
camp near Gibeah. The men of Israel went out
to fight the Benjamites and took up battle positions
against them at Gibeah. The Benjamites came
out of Gibeah and cut down twenty-two thousand
Israelites on the battlefield that day.

I am not an avid boxing fan. I am not even a halfhearted boxing fan. Hockey is my sport of choice, but I do know that there are "rounds" in boxing and a round lost does not solidify a loss of the entire match. Quite often in a boxing match you do lose a round or two; notwithstanding, the final decision goes in your favor.

In this fight for your faith you will stumble upon something similar. You may experience a period of time when you undergo defeat; and as you do, it is imperative for you remember that this defeat is only transitory. Victory *is* the final outcome for those who know who they are in Christ and you must be aware of this. A period of defeat may come your way, but it should not be allowed to make itself at home in your life.

In the twentieth chapter of Judges, we notice the Israelites suffered a loss on the battlefield even though they sought God before they went into this battle. Why would God lead them into a situation that would end in failure?

Previously, we noticed that faith was a fight and part of the definition of the word fight was "as if led." It is important for us to understand that at times God will lead us into a "round" or two of defeat for a precise reason; at times that reason is to prove our faith genuine. Defeat is a powerful instrument used for proving the authenticity of your faith. Faith is the substance of things *unseen*. Success does not require faith; success is the *end* result of faith while defeat is a facet of the progression of faith.

Habakkuk 2:2-3 (Ampl.) And the Lord answered me and said, Write the vision and engrave it so plainly upon tablets that everyone who passes may [be able to] read [it easily and quickly] as he hastens by. For the vision is yet for an appointed time and it

hastens to the end [fulfillment]; it will not deceive or disappoint. Though it tarry, wait [earnestly] for it, because it will surely come; it will not be behindhand on its appointed day.

Faith is a process; it takes time. God tells us in Habakkuk to write the Word and read it while we are waiting. The Hebrew word that "write" was translated from also means to prescribe. Prescribe means to set down, order, or advise. In writing down the vision we are declaring with authority the course of action we see according to the Word. We write down the vision which is according to God's Word – His promises for our specific need. We write the Word down so that we can *see* it, so that we can keep our focus on it; we write it down and make plain that God's promise is the end result of our situation. Writing the Word down and keeping our focus on it will change us. The Word will produce faith in us and that faith will bring the promises to pass, but the fulfillment of the promise is the *end* of the process. In between we will experience the fight for our faith.

When you feel as if you have sought God and made decisions based on His Word and His will and even still you are experiencing failure, you must understand that you are in the *middle* of your process. You are in the fight for your faith. What do you do?

John 6:68 (NIV)   Simon Peter answered Him, "Lord, to whom shall we go? You have the words of eternal life."

Peter came to the same realization we must come to: there is nowhere else to turn. Only Jesus Christ can give us the *Zoë* life we long for. Only the Word can bring the promises to pass that we are desperate for.

Do we give up during this fight? Giving up is not an option if your faith is genuine; the Word of God produces faith that endures. If you feel that you cannot press on do not degrade yourself – simply realize that God is making you aware of a need in your life, a need for more of His Word.

Judges 20:22 (NIV)   But the men of Israel encouraged one another and again took up their positions where they had stationed themselves the first day.

After the loss they endured, the Israelites encouraged one another. The impact and significance of encouragement cannot be stressed enough. A person who incessantly voices the negative is a drain on the listener. A Spiritually encouraging word can transform a situation and provide a person with the ammunition they need to once again join the battle. Encouragement enabled the Israelites to take their positions once more – the very same position they took the first day. Many times we feel defeated and as a result we decide that our course of action must have been wrong, but that is not always the case. Focusing on the Word is the correct procedure – no matter how long it may take for the promise to come to pass.

Experiencing defeat can be discouraging; therefore, you necessitate surrounding yourself with encouraging people. God will purposely allow us to go through these times; He may even allow us to go through several consecutive bouts of defeat. It is of the essence that you maintain the ability to take up your position *again*. If you cannot help being encompassed by negative people, then you must possess the ability to encourage yourself in the Lord. This ability will only be acquired through abiding in the encouragement found in the Word of God. Focus on verses that express victory and encouragement.

Defeat can breed doubt. An episode of defeat can give birth to enough reservation in your life to remove you from the fight for your faith entirely. While victory produces confidence, we must be sure the confidence is properly placed in Christ. The defeat, if understood correctly, can be used as a tool to draw us into greater dependence on God. If the Israelites would have won, then would they have been so quick to go and weep before the Lord and ask His opinion about going to battle again? Would they have been boastful in their victory? We must understand that whether we are winning or losing, our confidence must be placed wholly in Christ. Victory does not provide us with a reason to trust in ourselves. Any victory that we procure is only the result of our faith; therefore, we only have God to thank for the victory. Conversely, defeat does not provide us with a reason to give up on God. It is only a temporary setback.

Judges 20:23-25 (NIV) The Israelites went up and wept before the LORD until evening, and they inquired of the LORD. They said, "Shall we go up again to battle against the Benjamites, our brothers?" The LORD answered, "Go up against them." Then the Israelites drew near to Benjamin the second day. This time, when the Benjamites came out from Gibeah to oppose them, they cut down another eighteen thousand Israelites, all of them armed with swords.

Once again the Israelites sought the Lord and once again He instructed them to go to a losing battle, or so it would seem. We must take courage and be strengthened from these times of apparent defeat knowing that this is not permanent. Defeat is not failure; it is not eternal.

Psalms 34:19 (NIV)   A righteous man may have many troubles, but the LORD delivers him from them all.

God's plan is to deliver us; that is His will for our lives. Do not allow the circumstances that you encounter, before you see your deliverance, defeat you.

There will be times during this fight for your faith that you will feel defeat, and there will also be times when you feel like you are going backward.

Exodus 14:1-2 (Ampl.)   And the Lord said to Moses, Tell the Israelites to turn back and encamp before Pi-hahiroth, between Migdol and the [Red] Sea, before Baal-zephon. You shall encamp opposite it by the sea.

The Lord told Moses and the Israelites to *turn back and encamp* – go backward, stand still, and remain. Did you ever feel like you were going backward instead of forward? For instance, you may have been fighting depression and you began to experience joy and then suddenly you were more depressed than ever. If you feel like you are wandering in reverse, then you must open your eyes to what God desires to accomplish in your life. He took the Israelites back in order to give them a phenomenal victory; a victory that was no doubt something God brought about! At the time God directed them to turn back they were ahead of the Egyptians; if they outran them, then it would have been a victory of miniscule proportion. How miraculous would it have been if they would have outran them when they were already so far ahead? God wanted the Egyptians to catch up to the Israelites in order for the victory to be a miraculous one! God may be taking you backward right now, but remember the final outcome – a miraculous victory!

As a child of God we need to be trained, by the Word of God, to ignore our circumstances. We must look to the Lord instead of what is going on around us. There will be times in our lives when our circumstances are screaming out that God's promises will never be realized in our lives, but visual evidence is not always truth according to the Word of God. You may be experiencing temporary "defeat" in your life right now as you read this sentence but do not let it stop you!

Jeremiah knew what it was like to experience the "loss of a round."

> **Jeremiah 20:1-9 (Ampl.) Now Pashhur…heard Jeremiah prophesying these things. Then Pashhur beat Jeremiah the prophet and put him in the stocks…the next day Pashhur brought Jeremiah out of the stocks. Then Jeremiah said to him, The Lord does not call your name Pashhur [liberation], but**

Magor-missabib [terror on every side]. ...And you, Pashhur, and all who dwell in your house shall go into captivity; you shall go to Babylon, and there you shall die and be buried, you and all your friends to whom you have prophesied falsely. [But Jeremiah said] O Lord, You have persuaded and deceived me, and I was persuaded and deceived; You are stronger than I am and You have prevailed. I am a laughingstock all the day; everyone mocks me. For whenever I speak, I must cry out and complain; I shout, Violence and destruction! For the Word of the Lord has become to me a reproach and a derision and has brought me insult all day long. If I say, I will not make mention of [the Lord] or speak any more in His name, in my mind and heart it is as if there were a burning fire shut up in my bones. And I am weary of enduring and holding it in; I cannot [contain it any longer].

Jeremiah declares the Word of the Lord to Pashhur and his people. The word is not a word of victory or triumph but one of defeat. This word created problems for Jeremiah – this word that *God* gave him.

Did you ever feel like you were experiencing more problems because of the Word? Did *you* ever feel as if the promises that God gave you were the very cause of the trial that you were experiencing? Jeremiah felt "persuaded and deceived." He felt as if God had talked him into believing something that he would never receive. Perhaps God has persuaded you. Perhaps when you were studying His Word or when you were listening to a sermon or reading a book on His promises you were persuaded to believe something from His Word, but instead of moving forward and receiving the promise, you feel as if you are going farther away from the promise. You may wonder why God went through the trouble of persuading you only to let you down. You may feel deceived – you may feel like what God said in His Word is not the truth for *your* life! You may feel misinformed, mislead, and maybe even betrayed, but we have to understand that God *cannot* deceive us! Whatever He says *will* come to pass! When it takes time to come to pass that is when many give up and feel like they were deceived, but we must press on; we must take root in the Word. We must understand what is happening in our lives and what God is bringing to pass.

Through the power that Christ has bestowed upon you, you can look past your trial to the end result and you can press past the pain of the trial.

If truth be told, I am sure that every one of you reading this book knows what it means to feel what Jeremiah described as "persuaded and deceived." Even though you know what it means you have probably never shared this feeling. Many times we feel like a failure as a Christian if we have these feelings, but that is not true! We all have feelings and those feelings do not define us. We do not have to try to disguise our feelings. God is well aware of how we feel! Why do we believe we can deceive Him in regards to our feelings? We need to be honest with Him about our feelings if we are ever going to get past those feelings.

Moses also knew what it meant to feel persuaded and deceived and Moses spoke up about it (just like Jeremiah did).

> **Numbers 11:11-15 (Ampl.) And Moses said to the Lord, Why have You dealt ill with Your servants? And why have I not found favor in Your sight, that You lay the burden of all this people on me? Have I conceived all this people? Have I brought them forth, that You should say to me, Carry them in your bosom, as a nursing father carries the sucking child, to the land which You swore to their fathers [to give them]? Where should I get meat to give to all these people? For they weep before me and say, Give us meat, that we may eat. I am not able to carry all these people alone, because the burden is**

too heavy for me. And if this is the way You deal with me, kill me, I pray You, at once, and be granting me a favor and let me not see my wretchedness [in the failure of all my efforts].

Moses felt let down; he felt liked God misinformed him. God told him he would lead these people to freedom and it seemed as if anything but that was happening at the time. They may have been free from the Egyptians but they soon began to encounter a variety of other difficulties. Moses feels like he is far from God's favor; he feels burdened; he feels overwhelmed – to the point of wanting to die! Can you relate? Are you carrying a burden you cannot deal with – or even worse still, do you feel like you are dealing with it alone? Do you feel like God is dealing "ill" with you?

> ILL: to *spoil* (literally by *breaking* to pieces);
> figuratively to *make* (or *be*) *good for nothing*, that is, *bad* (physically, socially or morally). *Associate selves* and *show self friendly* - by mistake for something negative. Afflict, (be, bring, do) evil (doer, entreat, man), do harm, (do) hurt, do mischief, punish, still vex, (do) wicked (doer, -ly), be (deal, do) worse.

What a ghastly definition – Moses feels like God showed Himself friendly only to break him in pieces! He feels "persuaded and deceived." He feels like God was in relationship with him for the purpose of punishing and vexing him. What an appalling feeling! Do we recognize this feeling?

We must understand that we might have to go backward before we go forward but that does *not* mean God is dealing "ill" with us. It simply means that He is setting us up for a miraculous victory!

A man named Gideon could relate with losing ground – or should I say losing men (Judges 7:2). He started out with an army of thirty-two thousand men with which to go to battle but God had other plans.

God took Gideon's army from thirty-two thousand down to three-hundred in order to keep them from pride. God does not want us to mistake His miracle for something that we accomplished in our own strength. He knows that man can easily become prideful.

Deuteronomy 8:17 (Ampl.) And beware lest you say in your [mind and] heart, My power and the might of my hand have gotten me this wealth.

Wealth in this verse means anything from money to abilities. It is anything that is a blessing in your life; anything that adds to your life in an awe-inspiring way. Our hope needs to be in Christ alone.

If I can have even a little confidence in myself, then it takes me away from total dependence on Christ!

He will take us backward so that there is no mistaking Who gets the glory!

Gideon had too many people with him, Moses and the Israelites were too far ahead of the Egyptians, and then there is you and your situation. Do not allow regression to make you feel defeated. Losing ground can very well be the last step before your miraculous victory!

Another Biblical hero who was an example of losing a round or two was Isaac. Isaac was blessed by God. His wealth made others envy him and that envy made them come against him and what he was doing (Genesis 26:12-22).

People will not always be happy about your blessings (Mark 10:29-30). Are you shocked by this statement? Many times blessings come with persecutions but we have to walk in everything that God has for us regardless of others.

Isaac was blessed and then he moves on and begins to reopen the wells his father dug previously– as he does this, Isaac begins to experience something that opposes his blessing. He begins to experience defeat instead of victory. He begins to encounter opposition. Did he give up? No, he moved on! He moved on and continued to dig; we need to move on from our negative situations and continue to dig. Dig deeper into the Word! Find more proof for what you believe! Do not give up and you *will* reach your place of flourishing!

Many times the victory seems as elusive as finding the perfect diet and because of this we will hurt, we will doubt, and we will get angry – just to name a few! During this time we will experience a variety of feelings and it is important that we deal with them. Feeling as if God has deceived you is a feeling that you can try to bury but it will rear its ugly head repeatedly unless you come to terms with it. Too many times we decide that the feeling we are experiencing is just wrong instead of understanding that, wrong or not, it is a real feeling that must be addressed. Going in reverse is not something we will be overjoyed about so we need to accept the fact that we will have our ups and downs. No matter how we feel, we must understand that the Word of God is the *only* way out of the situation that we are in.

Some days it may even feel painful to read a promise that is totally contrary to your situation at the time, but push past the pain. We must declare, in the same way that Jeremiah did, "His Word is like a fire in me!" I cannot ignore the Word! I have to declare it! I have to read it! I cannot live without it!

Abiding in the Word will provide us with the faith necessary to withstand the trouble; it will produce the faith we need to be victorious. Anything is possible to the one who walks by faith!

What a list we find in the book of Hebrews describing what is accomplished by faith (Hebrews 11:32-35). Faith turns your trial into your victory! Faith makes us powerful in battle. Faith makes an army of enemies turn to flight.

Proverbs 16:7 (NIV) When a man's ways are pleasing to the LORD, He makes even his enemies live at peace with him.

We have found that faith is what pleases God (Hebrews 11:16) and we also know that our enemies are anything that is not in agreement with the Word. Any circumstance in our lives that is not in agreement with the Word of God is our enemy and all of our enemies must eventually live at peace with us when we are living by faith. During the fight for your faith you must understand that God is on your side; He wants these things that disagree with His Word to flee from you, too!

If we want to endure temporary defeat, then we must be full of faith; we must be full of the Word. The Word will enable us to be strong during the tough times. Faith is an amazing force that cannot be stopped; however, we can stop the production of faith in our lives by rejecting the Word of God.

As you fight for your faith and experience temporary defeat, keep in mind that these times are merely bumps in the road. I understand that bumps in the road may cause extensive damage but we must press on. A friend of ours suffered, at the hands of a major pot hole, four blown tires in one day! Despite her sufferings, she continues to drive. Those four tires were quite costly, it consumed most of her day having them changed, and she was not very pleased with the situation; nonetheless, she still continues to drive. If it seems silly for me to insinuate she would even consider giving up the act of driving, why then do we as Christians surrender when we encounter a "bump" in the road, even a bump that blows out all of our tires?

The Israelites went to God seeking an answer and He provided them with just that. We may be surprised by the answers God provides, especially when we are familiar with His promises. Experiencing defeat does not appear to coincide with the promised success the Bible boldly proclaims. In becoming acquainted with the promises we must also understand that these promises are only brought to pass by faith and patience – patience that may feel like the death of us at times!

Hebrews 6:12 (NIV) We do not want you to become lazy, but to imitate those who through faith and patience inherit what has been promised.

The journey of faith and patience includes the following: time, circumstances that do not line up with the promise, battles, conflicting thoughts, and the like. If you experience circumstances that are contrary to the Word, then refuse to give up! Patience is part of the process. Do not beat yourself up, either. You are not always the villain. If you are experiencing defeat it is not necessarily your fault; you may have been led to this place of defeat for the purpose of proving faith genuine. Even if it is your fault, there is nothing that you can do to change things; you require God's help no matter what brought your situation into being. Instead of trying to figure out what *you* did wrong, look to the Word on what God wants to do in your life!

2 Chronicles 20:9 (NIV) If calamity comes upon us, whether the sword of judgment, or plague or famine, we will stand in Your presence before this temple that bears Your Name and will cry out to You in our distress, and You will hear us and save us.

Jehoshaphat understood that the reason behind their state of affairs held no relevance. Jehoshaphat boldly declared that whether it was the sword of judgment or whether it was because of a plague or a famine, no matter what the reason was, they were going to stand in God's presence and call on Him for the help that they desperately required! We would be wise to do the same; we should be approaching God confident that He will hear us and He will help us! How many times do we find ourselves in a mess that was brought about by our own hand? No matter what the cause, Christ is the answer!

1 Samuel 12:14, 20 (Ampl.) If you will revere and fear the Lord and serve Him and hearken to His voice and not rebel against His commandment, and if both you and your king will follow the Lord your God, it will be good! And Samuel said to the people, Fear not. You have indeed done all this evil; yet turn not aside from following the Lord...

They had done "all this evil;" however they still had hope. We still have hope. God is not rejecting us because of the evil that we do. He is well aware that we need *Him* to keep us from evil. Do not allow evil to keep you away from Him! Do not attempt to hide from God in the same way that Adam and Eve did after they ate the fruit.

We only compound the problem by refusing to go to God for the help that we desperately require because of some silly notion that God will only help us if we were somehow "good enough" to be worthy of the assistance. We are then being arrogant enough to assume that there *are* times that we *do* warrant help.

It can never be reiterated enough that any Spiritual actions that we accomplish are only because of Christ; therefore, there will never be a time that we are *deserving* of God's help. His help is always a *gift*!

There are also those times when we have nothing to do with the trial that we are going through. In the same way a plague or famine is not something we can control or it is not something we bring on ourselves, some of our problems are because of "natural" occurrences. Problems with the economy, situations we are thrust into because of someone else, a natural disaster, and so on, are examples of "the plague or famine." No matter what comes your way, God is well-aware and well-able to take care of you. He knew about your need before you did.

Whether our problem is self-inflicted or beyond our control, we must quickly run to the *only* source of help we have; we must run to the Lord for the help we need with our trials!

The Israelites went through two devastating defeats before victory ensued. If they would have given up, then the victory would have never been experienced. Genuine faith will continue on; it cannot give up! The more we are abiding in the Word the more we will experience just such faith. Faith that will press on and see kingdoms conquered, justice administered, and promises gained. Faith that will shut the mouths of lions, quench the fury of the flames, and escape the edge of the sword. Faith that will turn our weakness into strength, make us powerful in battle and send the enemy running. You can have that kind of faith – faith that will turn death into life. Defeat does not have to be the end of you if you can understand its value.

2 Corinthians 4:17 (NIV) For our light and momentary troubles are achieving for us an eternal glory that far outweighs them all.

In the course of the fight for our faith we will encounter times, or even seasons, of defeat; we must understand that even these battles can serve a purpose. The defeat can work to our advantage if we keep our eyes on the end result. In Corinthians we find Paul describing our troubles as light and momentary *in comparison to* the glory (the manifestation of God's presence) which they achieve for us. The trials achieve an eternal glory; this glory will last forever. Eternal means perpetual; it is continuous or uninterrupted glory. If we focus on the trial rather than what it is working to achieve, then we will be tempted to surrender and we may even give in to that temptation. Our faith is worth fighting for; we are fighting for an eternal glory and we must keep that in mind. Whatever our faith produces lasts for eternity; these moments of defeat are temporary!

It is important for us to refrain from magnifying the defeat. To magnify means to make large, to make the center of attention. Many times in Scripture we find exhortations to magnify *the Lord*; in doing so we make *Him* our center of attention rather than our trials.

Psalms 69:30 (Ampl.) I will praise the name of God with a song and will magnify Him with thanksgiving.

We can magnify the Lord in many ways. Communicating His Word instead of our doubts and fears is an awesome way to magnify the Lord. Our words are significant; they are either magnifying God and His goodness or they are magnifying our problems. Praising the Lord, thanking the Lord, lifting His name up – all of these are ways to magnify God or make Him larger than the trials of life. Meditating on

His promises as opposed to our problems also magnifies the Lord. Magnifying the Lord, in any way, will always be the result of abiding in the Word.

The Word of God must be our priority if we are going to have the victory over the temporary defeat –or get through the loss of a round. There will be times when we have to lose ground before we can take possession of what God has for us; we have to be able to come to terms with such situations. We have to fill ourselves with the Word of God so that we can possess the genuine faith needed to overcome these discouraging times.

Chapter 7
FAITH IS FEARLESS

1 John 4:18-19 (NIV)
There is no fear in love. But perfect love drives out fear, because fear has to do with punishment. The one who fears is not made perfect in love. We love because He first loved us.

Many times when we experience a round of defeat fear quickly ensues. We begin to fear more loss or pain. Faith leaves no room for fear. Fear is the contradiction of faith; it is an absence of the Word.

> **Luke 8:50 (Ampl.) ...Do not be seized with alarm or struck with fear; simply believe [in Me as able to do this]...**

The answer for fear is faith, faith that is produced by abiding in the Word. Fearlessness, like faith, is not something we *decide* to possess.   We cannot muster up an attitude of courage on our own. In our key verse for this chapter we find that perfect love is what drives fear out. What is perfect love? It is the love that Jesus Christ bestows on us; it is *Spiritual* love. We can only love because He first loved us with this perfect love. Love that is found outside of Christ is not perfect; it is not complete. Love is made complete only through Christ.

1 John 4:16-17 (NIV) And so we know and rely on the love God has for us. God is love. Whoever lives in love lives in God, and God in him. In this way, love is made complete among us so that we will have confidence on the day of judgment, because in this world we are like Him.

This complete love, or Spiritual love, is experienced when we are abiding in Christ. He is perfect love and when we abide in Him that love is worked out through us. His love provides us with confidence; it does not promote fear! Complete love drives fear out because it reveals to us who we are *in Christ*. In this world, now – not when I get to heaven, I *am* like Christ! I am like Him because He loves me so much that He gave me *His* Spirit! His Spirit abides in me; it is the very essence of who He is. I have Christ in me; therefore, His characteristics can spring forth from me. I can be free of fear and I can walk in confidence when I walk in Christ, when I walk in who I am in Him. No longer do we need to fear judgment; our sins have been paid for and they are forgiven and forgotten – forever. I can be confident that my sins are no longer an issue. God is not forgiving me now only to bring my sin up to me later when I meet Him face-to-face. The blood of Jesus has cleansed me once for *all*. He paid the total price for my sin and my shame; there is no balance due by me!

Imperfect love fears punishment. Man focuses on fear; they use it against one another. Fear is even a popular vehicle in some churches, unfortunately. When people teach that we need to do "this" or God is going to do "that," we are instilling fear – a fear that eventually pushes people away from God. Why do some feel the need to scare people into what is only feigned obedience? They feel this need because they doubt that the Word alone can accomplish Spiritual actions in a child of God. It is incorrectly assumed that a little fear is good for us. Fear is not good for us. Fear is not Spiritual; therefore, fear cannot create Spiritual actions in us.

2 Timothy 1:7 (KJV) For God hath not given us the spirit of fear; but of power, and of love, and of a sound mind.

Fear is not from God; consequently, fear is sin. Fear is not Spiritual; we must recognize that it is of the flesh. It is a spirit from the enemy. Fear can only produce works of the flesh and those works do not count for eternity. Why would we assume that we could use a spirit from the enemy to produce Spiritual actions in a child of God? Looking at it this way draws attention to the absurdity; however, fear is being advocated from the pulpit.

Fear-based messages are preached in hopes of scaring people enough to keep them away from sin, but this never produces Spiritual fruit. For instance, singles are often taught to abstain from sex because of sexually transmitted diseases; however, the fear of a disease cannot produce *Spiritual* abstinence. This method of teaching is also employed by the world. Many health classes show videos of child birth hoping to scare girls away from sex; nevertheless, the teenage pregnancy rates continue to rise. Back in the church world, many continue to employ the fear message in vain attempts to transform their listeners. Some teach that you will never be able to have sexual relations with your husband or wife without thinking about the other person or persons you have had sex with prior to your spouse. This is also fear-based; it is not Word-based. Once again, fear cannot produce any Spiritual action in us. We can abstain from sex before marriage and it can be sin in God's eyes *if we are motivated by fear*. Anything that is not of faith is sin. Flesh can only give birth to flesh! We must understand this. Fear is a carnal source and it cannot produce a Spiritual action. *Spiritual* abstinence will only occur as the result of abiding in the Word.

These fear-based messages also promote the feeling of hopelessness in those who have already failed to abstain. A woman or man who has had premarital sex will feel hopeless in their marriage relationship because of statements like the one above. God does not promote hopelessness; His desire is for us to feel hopeful! God does not want you to think of your past and be paralyzed by it. In fact, He states that we will seldom think about our past because He will keep us occupied with gladness of heart (Ecclesiastes 5:20); He will fill us so full of joy that we do not have time to think about the negatives of the past! He wants us to let go of the past and press on to what is ahead. God can help us put our past out of mind if we let Him!

Why does God direct us to abstain from premarital sex? He wants us to experience the best! It is not in our best interest to have sex with more than one person. He is not going to hate us if we engage in premarital sex, but He knows that we may hate ourselves for a period of time if we do. God knows the repercussions we may have to experience as a result and He is instructing us based on what is best for us because of His indescribable love for us.

> **Deuteronomy 4:40 (NIV) Keep His decrees and commands, which I am giving you today, so that it may go well with you and your children after you and that you may live long in the land the LORD your God gives you for all time.**

Keeping your focus on the Word, not fear, makes it "go well with you." His love is what His Word is based on – not fear. God loves you so much that He wants your life to be a good one. He knows how sin affects you and that is why He warns you and provides you with the way out of it.

Psalms 119:11 (KJV) Thy Word have I hid in mine heart, that I might not sin...

God has provided us with His Word; it is our weapon against sin. We are to be encouraged by the Word and its ability to keep us from sin, but Satan has deceived some into believing that the Word is not enough. Satan has offered us fear as an ancillary weapon and many have accepted it. Even in our translation of the Bible you see the endorsement of fear. Words have been translated in such a way that they emphasize fear. Let us look at an example.

Matthew 5:29 (NIV) If your right eye causes you to sin, gouge it out and throw it away. It is better for you to lose one part of your body than for your whole body to be thrown into hell.

The word that was translated as "hell" causes confusion; it encourages fear. The word "hell" was used in place of the word *Gehenna*. *Gehenna* is a valley in Jerusalem that was turned into a trash heap because it was the place where people previously sacrificed their babies to a false god. It was a cursed place, no one in Jerusalem would build there; it is not the place of eternal damnation that we think of. Sin figuratively puts us in this garbage dump; it produces nothing of value in our lives. The Jews understood this; they knew what *Gehenna* was. When Jesus told them that sin would put them in a place of worthlessness, they could relate.

Jesus speaks of the right eye. The word translated as right refers to what we receive and the eye signifies vision. What are we receiving from the things we are focused on? If what we are focused on entices us to sin, then we must remove it. If anything causes us to ignore the Word of God, we must recognize it as rubbish and then cut if off from our lives. It is better to lose what keeps us from the Word than to live our lives in the worthlessness of the flesh.

Matthew 5:22 (NIV) But I say unto you, That whosoever is angry with his brother without a cause shall be in danger of the judgment: and whosoever shall say to his brother, Raca, shall be in danger of the council: but whosoever shall say, Thou fool, shall be in danger of hell fire.

Here we see another example of the misuse of the word "hell." Jesus was not saying that being upset with someone for no reason or calling them a fool (which is literally translated as blockhead) will send you to eternal damnation. He was simply stating that living this way will lead us to a place similar to the valley of *Gehenna*. We will find ourselves in a place comparable to the garbage dump, the place of death, because Jesus told us our flesh counts for nothing – it equals death (John 6:63). It is our flesh that makes us mad at someone for no reason; it is our flesh that insults others. It is our flesh that makes us commit *any and every* sin! Living in the flesh produces death; it counts for nothing and that is what He is communicating to us, but hell sounds much scarier. We may try to scare our kids into submission but God does not.

Matthew 10:28 (NIV) Do not be afraid of those who kill the body but cannot kill the soul. Rather, be afraid of the one who can destroy both soul and body in hell.

Here we are told not to fear a person who can physically kill us. Why? We do not need to fear them because we do not need to fear death. Why, then, would He go on to tell us to fear hell or eternal separation from Him? That does not make sense. In making sense of this we find that the words "the one" are added into the text; in the King James Version these two words are not found. Instead, the phrase, "him which," is found and it means a man or a woman; this phrase is *not* referring to God. It is a man or a woman that can destroy both soul and body in this place referred to as hell.

Hell, in this instance, once again refers to *Gehenna* - that place of cursing and worthlessness. It is not talking about an eternal separation from God. When we look at it as an eternal separation from God it induces fear. We must look at this the right way, the way Jesus said it. We do not have to be afraid of death. What we should be afraid of is our flesh. The "which," the man or woman, is us! We should be afraid of allowing our flesh to thrive because in doing so *we* make our lives miserable. No one can kill your soul (your mind, your will, your emotions) except you! People may try, but we are the ones who must allow it to happen. We are the ones who put ourselves in this place translated as hell, the place of the flesh.

Hell is translated for three words in the Bible and only one of them is the actual word for eternal damnation. Why? Why use this word that means eternal damnation? It is used because fear is a powerful tool! Regrettably, it is an evil tool.

We need to live free of fear; we must refrain from beliefs that instill fear. The fear factor must be removed from the church! Fear is a tool of the devil and it has no place in the church. When we bring fear into the church we are giving the devil a foothold. Keep in mind that Satan will even try to use the Word against us.

John 14:15 (KJV) If ye love Me, keep My commandments.

The above verse has also been improperly used to inflict fear on the listener. Fear of not loving God enough is paralyzing! If we believe that our love for God can make us perfect, then we must also believe that we do not love God when we sin. This way of thinking can lead us into incapacitating depths of loneliness, guilt, and fear – and when we need God the most, we will feel as if we do not deserve His love, compassion, and support. This is devastating. We must understand the true meaning of this verse. We do this by digging into the original text. The word "keep," as we have already discussed, is translated from the Hebrew word *shamar* which means to focus on, hedge about as with thorns, and act as a watchman. It is not referring to living a faultless life. Loving God is the result of God loving us; not the result of our specious perfection. We love Him because He first loved us.

1 John 4:10 (NIV) This is love: NOT that we loved God, but that He loved us and sent His Son as an atoning sacrifice for our sins.

What is love? It is not an action that originates with man; it originates with God. True love is the love that God has for us. The love that God gives us enables us to keep our focus on His love letter. We guard the Word in our lives because we understand its value. God's love enables us to hedge the Word in our lives; it keeps everything contrary to the Word out of our lives – including fear!

John 15:14 (NIV) You are My friends if you do what I command.

The Word enables us to put the Word into practice in our lives. A friend is a companion; it is someone who spends times with you. As we spend time in the Word we will find ourselves doing more of what the Word says and less of what our flesh entices us to do. The word "do" actually means to abide or agree. A friend of the Word abides in it and agrees with it because their consistent intake of the Word produces faith. A companion of the Word is in agreement with the Word and their lives manifest that agreement. This verse is not meant to scare us into perfect living or make us feel guilty; it is meant to empower us by encouraging us to live in Christ!

If we are focused on the Word of God, then fear does not have a chance. Fear only abounds where faith does not.

Luke 1:68, 74-75 (NIV) Praise be to the Lord, the God of Israel, because He has come and has redeemed His people…to rescue us from the hand of our enemies, and to enable us to serve Him without fear in holiness and righteousness before Him all our days.

The Word of God informs us that we have been redeemed. To be redeemed is to be seen again as God intended. His original purpose for us was to be created in His image. We have been redeemed from our lives of sin by the blood of the Lamb. We are seen again as the righteousness of God compliments of Jesus Christ. Sin no longer stands between us and God. Our lives are hidden through Christ; when God looks at us He sees Jesus. Our intimate knowledge of this enables us to serve God fearlessly! It allows us to serve Him through Christ without feeling inadequate. Serving Him in righteousness and holiness can only be done when we are in agreement with what the Word says about who we are in Christ. On our own we have no righteousness; we are only holy because He is holy. Attempting to serve Him outside of who we are in Christ will lead to frustration and failure. Serving God is a Spiritual action – it requires the Spiritual Seed of God's Word. He is not served by *human* hands (Acts 17:25).

Fear kicks in when we are ignorant of our Spiritual identity in Christ. Christ is our fearlessness! In the Word we are told to come to God through Christ. Tacking "in Jesus' name" onto the end of our prayers mindlessly minimizes the meaning of coming to God through Christ. We can only enter the presence of God through Christ. On our own we lack the ability to approach the throne. We must come to God presenting all that Christ is and all that He has done for us, thus procuring our access to God. Jesus is the way to the Father; we cannot draw near to God without Him! When we present Christ and all that He has accomplished for us, we can then go boldly to the throne and expect God to do what He has promised.

Perfect love casts out fear. If we are going to live a fearless life, then we are going to have to live in the love God has for us. We are to remain conscious of His love; we do this by reminding ourselves daily through the Word. This is a process that takes time – time that is worth the investment.

Chapter 8
FAITH AND PATIENCE

Hebrews 6:12 (NIV)
**We do not want you to become
lazy, but to imitate those who through faith and
patience inherit what has been promised.**

Faith is a process; it is to be our way of life. The promises of
God will be realized in our lives in time as we walk by faith. It
takes faith and patience.

I find it interesting that laziness is identified as the
contradiction of faith and patience. A study of the word "lazy"
reveals that this word comes from the Greek word *nothros*.
This word is derived from the word for an illegitimate son.
Nothros is defined as sluggish, that is, (literally) lazy, or
(figuratively) stupid, dull, slothful.

We know that faith is the result of abiding in the Word;
therefore, if we are lazy with the Word faith will not be
produced. Laziness with the Word inhibits the production of
faith.

If you recall, the word "understand" had to do with
your association or companionship with Christ. Proverbs,
chapter fifteen and verse fourteen, told us that the mind of him

who has understanding seeks knowledge, inquires after it, and craves it. Understanding is a contradiction to laziness. Laziness with the Word comes from a lack of understanding; its roots lie in feelings of illegitimacy. A person who is lazy with the Word is a person who lacks knowledge or understanding regarding their Spiritual identity. Laziness with the Word is a derivative of ignorance, ignorance of your Spiritual identity.

What makes a person lazy with the Word? I believe the word that *nothros* is derived from gives us an answer. I have found that an erroneous view of who you are in Christ is directly related to your use of the Word. Far too many Christians do not occupy their rightful position as sons and daughters and they live as illegitimate children. A person who is insecure in their Spiritual identity is usually under condemnation when they read the Word of God. They do not comprehend that the Word of God is written to two different groups of people: saved and unsaved. They have trouble distinguishing between the two. They will apply things that are addressed to the unsaved to themselves because they do not understand what is theirs in Christ; they do not rightly divide what is addressed to the Spiritual person from what is addressed to the carnal. For instance, they will fear judgment even though God has said that their sins are as far as the east is from the west (Psalms 103:12) if they are His child. People who read the Word of God in this manner will eventually begin to ignore it.

The Bible informs us that the just will live by faith; however, if we do not believe that we are just, why would we then believe that we should live by faith? An understanding of who you are is vital in this Spiritual life we are meant to live.

Laziness with the Word can be the result of ignorance. Ignorance is nothing more than a lack of knowledge. As a Christian we must recognize the Word of God for what it is in our life.

Deuteronomy 32:47 (NIV) They are not just idle words for you--they are your life. By them you will live long in the land you are crossing the Jordan to possess.

The Word of God is our life! Do we classify it with such magnitude? Is it of crucial significance to us? The Word of God is visibly overlooked in the world; but unfortunately, it is overlooked in Christianity, as well. Many times Christians try everything but the Word to solve their problems when the Word is in fact the only answer. The Word will take us into the life that we long to live and it will enable us to maintain that life. Without the Word we will simply exist and we will do so miserably. If we do not recognize the value of the Word, then we will not employ it in our lives. God has told us that

His Word produces faith; faith will keep us out of sin, it will bring about the promises in our lives, it will defeat Satan's attack, it will give us the victory, and it will produce Spiritual fruit in our lives. What else could we possibly ask for? All throughout Scripture He reiterates the importance and value of the Word.

Laziness can also be the outcome of over-committing yourself to everything else that life has to offer. "I'm so busy!" seems to be the normal response when asked, "How are you?" When did "busy" become our position and depiction in life? Rest is a four-letter word to many people today.

According to God, the Word is my life; therefore, if I do not have the time to read the Word, I do not have time for a Spiritual life!

Making time to read the Word is not an option; it is a necessity, but people who are busy are usually too tired at the end of the day to add one more thing to their list. We first must understand that the Word is not something to *add* to our list; it must be our priority. The Word must come first; it is our life. We would not put off any other life-giving activity. Once again, this takes us back to ignorance. Do we really understand what God is articulating when He informs us that His Word is our life?

If I am too busy for the Word, then I must also believe that I am too busy to avoid sin, too busy to inherit the promises, too busy to walk in victory, too busy to defeat my flesh, and so on!

First Samuel chapter eight, verses ten through twenty-two, refers to laziness with the Word. The people decided that they wanted a king. They wanted a king to govern them and fight for them because they were too lazy to do these things for themselves. The people had God as their king, but when He was their king they had responsibility. The people did not want this accountability; they wanted someone else to be in charge for them. They did not want to prepare for the battle; they did not want to fight the battles. They did not even care what the end result of this laziness would be. They would lose what was theirs in the same way that we forfeit what is ours in Christ when we refuse to abide in the Word and prepare for the fight of faith.

No matter what the reason is for the laziness, the outcome is the same. If we identify a problem of laziness with the Word, then we can be sure that it needs to be rectified. Part of the definition of lazy is stupid or dull; it is stupid to ignore the Word of God when it provides you with everything you need for life and godliness. How many people are suffering because of problems that the Word of God can solve? The Bible is our answer! God's Word was sent to us to heal us in every area we need a healing.

Christians who do not live in the Word of God are not living a life where faith is abounding; therefore, promises are not being inherited. What about the Christians who are abiding in the Word? What about faith *and* patience?

Faith and patience inherit the promises. Faith, once again, is produced only through abiding in the Word of God; we cannot repeat this enough. This genuine Biblical faith will produce patience.

Romans 8:25 (NIV) But if we hope for what we do not yet have, we wait for it patiently.

Hope is confident expectation or faith; it is blind evidence. When we are certain of that which we believe, we *can* wait with patience. Impatience becomes a factor at what time doubt becomes an issue. Doubt creeps in and we begin to wonder if we are ever going to see the promise come to pass in our lives and accordingly we become annoyed and want God to speed things up for us. Genuine faith can wait; it is certain that what God has promised will come to pass. It is certain only because of the Word. If we begin to doubt any promise that God has made, then at that time we must immediately run to the Word for more proof or more evidence regarding God's promise to us because we need more faith and patience.

> **Hebrews 10:35-37 (NIV) So do not throw away your confidence; it will be richly rewarded. You need to persevere so that when you have done the will of God, you will receive what He has promised. For in just a very little while, "He who is coming will come and will not delay."**

Do not throw away your confidence – we do this by refusing to ignore the Word. We must hold on to the Word so that we can walk by faith. This is the will of God – and if you will hold on to the Word and wait for God's timing, then you *will* see the promise come to pass in your life.

> **Habakkuk 2:3 (NIV) For the revelation awaits an appointed time; it speaks of the end and will not prove false. Though it linger, wait for it; it will certainly come and will not delay.**

Bear in mind that the promise or the revelation speaks of the end. As discussed in a previous chapter, the fulfillment of the promise is the end of the *process* of faith in your life. It takes faith *and* patience to see the promises of God manifested in our lives – we must wait, but we must wait connected to the

Word of God. The Hebrew word that was translated as "wait" means to adhere. We must connect ourselves to the promises of God – that is Biblical waiting. If we are ignoring the Word but hoping that something changes in our situation, then we are not waiting Biblically – we are wasting our time.

It will take time for your promise to come to pass, but no matter how long it takes you must refuse to give up; it will come to pass. Refusing to give up will be the *fruit* of abiding in the Word of God, the specific Word referring to your situation.

Abiding in the Word will give us confidence in the Word. The Word is our confidence!

Jeremiah 17:7-8 (NIV) But blessed is the man who trusts in the LORD, whose confidence is in Him. He will be like a tree planted by the water that sends out its roots by the stream. It does not fear when heat comes; its leaves are always green. It has no worries in a year of drought and never fails to bear fruit.

Our confidence is richly rewarded – just look at the benefits in these verses from Jeremiah! Confidence means to trust in, be confident or sure, to be bold, secure and careless. Without a doubt, feelings such as these only come from making the Word of God our home. Our ability to persevere is directly related to the amount of God's Word we are storing up. We can wait with patience only when we are connected to the Word. Our confidence that is properly placed in Christ will enable us to prevail.

Have you ever recorded a sporting event only to find out the score before you had the chance to watch the recording? If you have, then you know what it is like to watch the game already knowing the end result. If you know that your team procures the victory, then no matter what happens during the game you will remain positive – positive that your team will win! You will not be depressed when the other team scores; even if they are in the lead you will not be bothered. No matter what takes place during the game you are still confident. I do believe that faith and patience can be equated to this same scenario. Confidence comes from knowing the end result.

Isaiah 46:10 (NIV) I make known the end from the beginning, from ancient times, what is still to come. I say: My purpose will stand, and I will do all that I please.

The Word declares the end result, do we know it? Do we live accordingly?

In Hebrews we found that after we do the will of God we will receive what He has promised. Keep in mind our key verse for this chapter: faith and patience bring about the promises. The will of God for our lives is to live by faith; therefore, doing the will of God is living by faith or living in the Word of God. Living in the Word will produce Spiritual actions, but do not be misled into believing that these actions are earning the promises. This bears repeating. Too many Christians fall into this trap and there are two outcomes: either you feel proud of what you *think* you have earned, or you give up because you feel like you cannot be good enough to receive from God.

Doing the will of God is not some attempt to be perfect on my part; it is living by faith or living dependent on the Word of God!

Patience never seems attractive to our flesh, but it is an attribute of the Holy Spirit and we *can* see it displayed in our lives. It may not be our favorite fruit, but it is significant. We necessitate it if we long for the promises. God will be true to His Word no matter what; patience is the key to seeing the promises come to pass in your life!

Patience is not for the weak. Abiding in the Word of God will give us the strength we need to be the "tough one" in this fight for our faith and it will enable us to endure with patience!

Proverbs 18:14 (Ampl.) The strong spirit of a man sustains him in bodily pain or trouble, but a weak and broken spirit who can raise up or bear?

Our Spirit needs to be strong – we need to build up our Spirit and we do this by abiding in the Word. When we do not abide in the Word we are weak Spiritually. Spiritual weakness leads to an ashamed, confused, and disappointed life – a life that is dry, withered and confounded. We know that God describes the Word as water; our lives are dry without the Word. Without the Word we live a withered life – one that is wasting away. We are also living a confounded life – a baffling, annoying, and irritating life. Shame, confusion, and disappointment await us when we ignore the Word and who can bear that?

A strong spirit sustains us in the pain or trouble caused by our flesh – that is the "bodily" pain or trouble. We will encounter pain from the flesh during this fight for our faith. We need strength! Our spirit is strengthened by the Word we deposit into it. More Word equates to more strength!

We can be strong or we can be weak. Spiritual weakness is the result of ignoring the Word and it will affect every area of your life. When we ignore the Word, we are left with only our flesh to draw from – and our flesh is weak, to say the least. It is an absence of Spirit.

> **Exodus 6:1-9 (Ampl.) Then the Lord said to Moses, *Now* you shall *see* what I will do to Pharaoh; for [compelled] by a strong hand he will [not only] let them go, but he will drive them out of his land with a strong hand. And God said to Moses, I am the Lord. I appeared to Abraham, to Isaac, and to Jacob as God Almighty [El-Shaddai], but by My name the Lord [Yahweh--the redemptive name of God] *I did not make Myself known to them [in acts and great miracles]*. I have also established My covenant with them...Moses told this to the Israelites, but they refused to listen to Moses because of their impatience and anguish of spirit and because of their cruel bondage.**

The Israelites did not want to hear what Moses had to say because they were Spiritually weak at this point. They were not walking by faith. They were focused on their situation instead of God's promise.

God had good things in store for them but they could not see past their present situation. He did not make Himself known to them in acts and great miracles at first, but things were about to change – sounds like faith and patience to me! He first established a covenant with them; the covenant is His Word. It is the same today. First, we receive the Word, not acts or great miracles. We have to believe before we see!

Hebrews 10:32 (Ampl.) But be ever mindful of the days gone by in which, after you were first spiritually enlightened, you endured a great and painful struggle.

The Word of God will be put to the test in the lives of everyone who walks by faith. After we are spiritually enlightened (after we receive the *implanted* Word) we go through a testing of faith. Do not think it is strange when you go through the trial – understand it is part of living by faith! Make up your mind to focus on the Word during the time of testing and you will stand firm. Remember the end result – set the joy before you. The Word will be proved true in your life if you will cling to the Word and wait on God.

It is essential for us to recognize that throughout the wait they were still being taken care of – remember the birds – they do not sow yet the heavenly Father takes care of them (Matthew 6:26)! The same is true of us; we are taken care of countless times when we do not sow the seed of faith regarding our care. How many of us are abiding daily in promises concerning our employment, our finances, our health, and so on; yet, the Heavenly Father is imparting to us the very thing we need. In the same way, they had the provision of their temporary residence but God wanted so much more for them; what He had for them would take faith! They, just like us, would have to sow the seed of the Word if they wanted to take hold of more.

The Israelites were promised awesome promises by God Himself but they did not want to hear them. Why? They did not want to listen to His promises because of their impatience, anguish of spirit, and their cruel bondage. Faith and patience inherit the promises; impatience ignores the promises! The waiting aspect of every trial tests the origination of your faith – if you can wait, then you posses the living faith that can only come from the Word of God.

Patience, just like faith, is the result of the Word. The ability to wait patiently for what God promised is the result of the work that the Word does in the life of the believer.

The Israelites did not want to hear about God's promises because they were tired of waiting! Are you tired of waiting? Are you turning a deaf ear to God's promises because you feel like you have been waiting forever? "Anguish of spirit" is also impatience; and, impatience is detrimental.

Along with impatience, they also suffered from cruel bondage. Whenever you endure a trial for an extended period of time, you begin to feel as if you are in bondage. Bondage is cruel – feelings of restriction do not exactly make us feel pleasant. These feelings intensify our lack of patience – we cannot wait to be free from the burden of the trial and escape the problem that seems to be imprisoning us. A trial that seems to go on forever will only magnify our lack of patience if we do not focus on the Word. For example, if we believe God in the area of prosperity but we can hardly wait as it is for Him to bless us financially, then a financial burden added to the equation only magnifies our impatience. We must fill ourselves with the Word.

Patience is produced as we go through our trials *with* the Word of God. We must understand that trials can be met with the Word. Too many times we let the trial choke the Word.

Previously, we pointed out that the Word of God is our seed and it can be suffocated or choked; it can be restricted from growth (Luke 8:14). If we do not look at our trials in a Biblical way, then they will choke the Word in our lives – we will not hear the Word, we will not take it in and make it part of who we are, and it will not affect our lives!

Trials must be viewed as opportunities to feed on the Word rather than reasons to avoid the Word. Every trial that you encounter can be met with God's promises on the subject.

Numbers 14:9 (KJV) Only rebel not ye against the LORD, neither fear ye the people of the land; for they [are] bread for us: their defense is departed from them, and the LORD [is] with us: fear them not.

The people were standing in their way of what God promised them. They represented the enemy, the trial, or anything that is contrary to the Word in our lives. We need to look at the enemy or the trial as an opportunity to "eat!" Open the Word and find as many verses as you can on the subject that you are dealing with and gobble them up. Eat until you are full; eat until the Word is coming back out of you! When you start to get the least little bit hungry, eat again! We do not have to worry about overeating where the Word is concerned!

We can walk in patience in spite of our circumstances *if* we abide in the Word of God. The Word of God will produce patience in us! Thank God for His Word!

Chapter 9
BROKEN FAITH

Malachi 2:14-16 (NIV)

You ask, "Why?" It is because the LORD is acting as the witness between you and the wife of your youth, because you have broken faith with her, though she is your partner, the wife of your marriage covenant. Has not the LORD made them one? In flesh and spirit they are His. And why one? Because He was seeking godly offspring. So guard yourself in your spirit, and do not break faith with the wife of your youth. "I hate divorce," says the LORD God of Israel, "and I hate a man's covering himself with violence as well as with his garment," says the LORD Almighty. So guard yourself in your spirit, and do not break faith.

Faith was not made to be broken. To prevent the breaking of our faith we require Spiritual protection.

What is the phrase "guard yourself in Spirit" referring to? These words were originally defined as "take heed to your Spirit" which means we are to guard our Spirit, protect it, focus on it, and hedge it in our lives as with thorns. We are to be very protective of our Spiritual identity. This phrase also indicates serving as a watchman of our Spirit. A watchman, at the time the Bible was written, would more readily die than lose what he was guarding (Acts 16:27). Do we guard our Spirit and the things of the Spirit with such vigilance? Our Spirit, in essence, is who we are in Christ; it is our Spiritual identity, our Spiritual ability. To guard yourself in Spirit you must be an avid student of the Word of God. The Word makes us intimately aware of who we are in Christ, thus protecting our Spiritual identity. Our attention to the Word will shield us from anything that comes against our Spirit.

We are told, "Do not break faith." This phrase is originally defined as "deal not treacherously;" this simply means do not act deceitfully or covertly – do not cover up or be unfaithful. The act of breaking faith is being untrue to who you are Spiritually. It is acting covertly, keeping your Spiritual identity a secret by living like the rest of the world even though you were created to be so much more. Living like the world does not merely refer to carousing like the world. What about those who complain like the rest of the world? What about those who live fearful the way the majority of the people do? What about those who wait in the grocery store line and are of the same mind as those who are talking about high prices and going broke? These are examples of people who are breaking faith, also. They are living like the unbelieving while "secretly" they are more than conquerors (Romans 8:37), "secretly" they do not have to fear anything or anyone

(Hebrews 13:6), and "secretly" they have a God who promises to prosper them even if the rest of the world is in a time of famine (Psalms 37:19)! When we live as if we do not have the promises of God, we are living covert lives; we are undercover Christians or faith-breakers.

In Malachi we see breaking faith equated to divorce in the English translation. The Hebrew word this was translated from is *shalach*. The Hebrew word for divorce is *garish*; this word is first used in Genesis chapter three, verse twenty-four. The King James version translated *garish* as "drove out." The Hebrew word *shalach* means to push away, send away, give up, and let depart. When we break faith He compares it to giving up or pushing away who we are in the Spirit. He has given us His Spirit because God is seeking Godly offspring. He gave mere man, who *was* entirely flesh, His Spirit in order for us to be Godly offspring. Our God is amazing!

Those who were far have been brought near through Christ. My flesh is no longer able to keep me from God because of what Christ has done in me; the barrier has been destroyed! Praise God!

I have the privilege of living Spiritually because I have His Spirit in me; I cannot be Spiritual on my own apart from Christ. A Christian who chooses to live their life in the flesh instead of the Word of God is a person who "breaks faith with the wife of their youth;" they separate themselves from their

Spiritual identity; they give up or push away who they are in Christ.

Breaking faith is conducting ourselves like the unsaved when in reality we are mighty and we possess all in Christ. Super heroes usually keep their "super" identities hidden and lead a normal life as a regular person; in the same way, many Christians live like the world. They behave like an unbeliever until they walk into the church where they then turn on their "super-powers." "Praise the Lord!" is the familiar lingo and a smile is always present; they float through the church as if on a cloud, not understanding that super-powers are not solely for the church services. Once they are back in the world doom and gloom overpower. "My life stinks and I just do not understand it," becomes the phrase of the day while they drudgingly walk on as if the weight of the world is on their shoulders. While they should be displaying their super-powers in this lost world, they are instead living like mere mortals and refusing to display the awesomeness of Christ. Instead of giving people something to hope in, they are joining the hopeless. Broken faith leads to broken lives; people who depart from who they really are in Christ. Once again this is the after-effect of ignoring the Word of God. How can I know who I am in Christ if I close my eyes to His Word?

God informs us that we cover ourselves with violence as well as with our garment; we clothe ourselves with unrighteousness, oppression, cruelty, and injustice in the same way we put our clothes on every day. Ignoring the Word and who you are in Christ is nothing more than being cruel to yourself. You are destroying your life by forfeiting all that Christ died to give you. In the Word you will discover countless promises that are yours in Christ; they are *already* yours. It is up to you to "put them on." We can be deprived of what is ours by ignoring the Word. God will not force His Word or His promises on any of us.

Each day we make a decision to put on clothing; in the same way, we must decide to put on who we are in Christ daily.

Colossians 3:9-10 (NIV) Do not lie to each other, since you have taken off your old self with its practices and have put on the new self, which is being renewed in knowledge in the image of its Creator.

The Word of God is truth; *a lie is anything that opposes the Word of God.* We are lying to ourselves and to each other when we identify with something that opposes the Word. If we want to tell each other the truth, then we must speak to each other according to the Word. We should not address ourselves or anyone else in a manner that is contrary to the Word. We must not address someone as a "loser" due to the fact that the Bible speaks of our worth and value in Christ. If I call someone a loser, then I am, in reality, lying to them. Take the time to look up the verses that have to do with lying and look at them in light of this understanding: a lie is anything that opposes the Word of God. Speak the truth – speak the Word!

In putting on the new self I am also putting off the old self. I will refuse to identify with my flesh when I am identifying with who I am in Christ. It is impossible for me to see myself as a loser *and* a person of worth and value simultaneously.

I must fill myself with the Word if I am going to view myself in keeping with the Word. The Word is what destroys wrong attitudes and identities. As I begin to ingest the Word of God my thoughts will begin to line up with the Word that is being stored in my heart.

Do you realize who you are in Christ? Are you in agreement with what God's Word says about you? Are you in agreement with God's promises for your life?

Let us look at some examples of the blessings God has bestowed on us as His children and discover our attitude toward each. For instance, God sent His Son to become your righteousness. Do you believe that you are the righteousness of God in Christ?

1 Corinthians 1:30-31 (NIV) It is because of Him that you are in Christ Jesus, who has become for us wisdom from God--that is, our righteousness, holiness and redemption. Therefore, as it is written: "Let him who boasts boast in the Lord."

Jesus Christ is my righteousness; when I choose to put on unrighteousness I oppress myself. I am "covering myself with violence." In identifying with unrighteousness I keep myself down; I do not live up to the life that Christ died for me to have. Believing that I am worthless and that I am unholy does not benefit me and it is in no way Spiritual. It is an act of breaking faith. I am giving up the righteousness that Christ died to give me!

Romans 8:1-2 (NIV) Therefore, there is now no condemnation for those who are in Christ Jesus, because through Christ Jesus the law of the Spirit of life set me free from the law of sin and death.

Now there is no condemnation, not when you achieve perfection because you never will! Jesus Christ set us free! Do not break faith and live as if you are under condemnation. Broken faith truly will lead to a broken life. Condemnation is a burden that no one is capable of bearing. You must guard your Spirit by focusing on the Word of God and coming to the realization that you are completely forgiven and condemnation is no longer relevant.

Psalms 18:23 (Ampl.) I was upright before Him and blameless with Him, ever [on guard] to keep myself free from my sin and guilt.

The Psalmist guarded his Spirit. He knew who he was Spiritually; he was upright *before Him* and blameless *with Him.* The Psalmist did not focus on who he was *outside of God* and he was on guard to stay away from the things of his flesh – namely, sin and guilt! Countless Christians are more than eager to associate with their sin and guilt. Pity parties, guilt trips, and the like, are "enjoyed" by Christians everywhere. We are breaking faith as a result of fellowshipping with such things – things of the flesh. Forgiveness is rightfully ours in Christ and we must walk in it if we are going to live the life of a victorious Christian. Focus on who you are in Christ. When you are tempted to mull over your sin be reminiscent of Christ's forgiveness; turn your pity party into a praise party. The Bible informs us that praise silences the enemy (Psalms 8:2); Satan will refrain from reminding you of your sin if you consistently convert it into a praise party that gives God glory!

Another Spiritual blessing that is bestowed on us is victory. Jesus Christ promises us the victory. Do you live in agreement with this promise? Do you expect victory in your life or are you anticipating loss and defeat?

The Christian who wanders through this life fearful of defeat is breaking faith. They are separating themselves from who they are and what is theirs in Christ.

1 John 5:4 (NIV) **For everyone born of God overcomes the world. This is the victory that has overcome the world, even our faith.**

Your faith will conquer *anything* that comes against you. It is your right as a child of God to conquer and be victorious. You have been promised victory and you can receive it!

Ephesians 6:16 (NIV) In addition to all this, take up the shield of faith, with which you can extinguish all the flaming arrows of the evil one.

Receive – take up your shield of faith! Let the Word go before you into battle. You can defeat anything that comes against you when you do!

In the same way that Jesus defeated Satan, we can defeat and gain the victory over *everything*. Satan wants us to doubt God's promises; he is well aware that a shortage of faith is equivalent to defeat. We must remain focused on the promises of God. Guard yourself in Spirit and hedge the Word of God in your life. Do not allow anything to touch the Word in your life. A person who guards themselves in Spirit will not tolerate separation from the Word due to their problems; they will not allow disappointment to keep them from praying *again*, they will not permit their thoughts to *continue* in contradiction to the Word, they will not allow anything to *chronically* impede them from the things of the Spirit.

God has also bestowed blessings on our family. In His Word He repeatedly makes mention of the good things that He has in store for our descendents and their descendents, as well. The person who is guarding their Spirit will hold fast to these promises.

> **Isaiah 49:25 (NIV) But this is what the LORD says: "Yes, captives will be taken from warriors, and plunder retrieved from the fierce; I will contend with those who contend with you, and your children I will save."**

Faith brings about His promises and faith comes from the Word – and faith produces patience. Do not break faith by giving up on your children. Time is not an issue for God. No matter how long it may take, do not give up – remain focused on His promises. God is faithful and He promises to save your children. Captives are taken from warriors when God is involved; in other words, the impossible is possible! Our children seem to provide us with many challenges as we attempt to raise them and these challenges may seem impossible, but with God they are not! Each challenge must be met with God's promised victory at the forefront. He will deliver your children; believe it!

God has also promised us that He hears our prayers. Are you in agreement with this promise? Do you believe that God is listening to you?

Psalms 17:6 (NIV) I call on You, O God, for You will answer me; give ear to me and hear my prayer.

We can rest assured knowing that God hears our prayers. There would be no motivation to pray if we believed that God was not listening. If we begin to have reservations, then we will probably abstain from prayer and prayer is essential in our lives – it is our method of communication with God. If you begin to doubt that God hears your prayers, then focus on the verses that proclaim that He is listening – fight back!

There will be times, especially during the fight for your faith, when you will feel as if God is not listening; during these times you must put your feelings aside and focus on the Word. Push past your feelings that are lying to you and persistently pray! Ignore your flesh and do what the Spirit is leading you to do. If you have a promise as your endorsement, then continue on in the Word and in prayer until that promise comes to pass; God is not a liar. Our flesh wants to give up and Satan would love for us to do just that; conversely, our Spirit is crying out to press on – and we can press on through Christ!

We repeatedly hear messages on prayer as Christians and in some of these messages we are supplied with qualifications for answered prayer. Understand that though these are well-meaning messages, they can be misleading. Speakers will list qualifications from revealing concealed sin to treating your spouse correctly; and to be honest, the qualifications are overwhelming. We must understand that "Christ in me" is the only qualification necessitated for answered prayer. When we begin to make lists, in essence, what we are doing is saying that we can *earn* an answer to our prayer. I understand that there are verses in His Word that speak about things that hinder our prayers, but if we refrain from surface reading and dig a little deeper I believe we will find something very interesting.

Anything that we are directed to do in the Word of God can only be performed in *one* way – through Christ by faith. I cannot perform a Spiritual action apart from Christ (He is the Word). If my actions have any other source, then they are sin. The Word of God is the source of faith; therefore, the Word of God (Jesus Christ) must be the source of my actions.

When the Word of God is first in our lives, our lives will testify. For example, I will treat my spouse in a way that is in accordance with the Word when I am walking in the Spirit. Only the Spirit gives birth to Spirit. If I try to treat my spouse nicer to earn a blessing, then I can be sure that I am walking in the flesh. I need the Word; in other words, I need Christ! Apart from Christ I can do nothing – nothing of Spiritual value. Similarly, my prayers will be hindered if I am coming to God outside of Christ – there will be no Spiritual value in my prayer if I go apart from Christ. If I go to God boasting about how well I treat my spouse and how I deserve to have my prayer heard, then I can be sure again that I am in the flesh.

We must understand something: Sin does not *hInder* my faith; sin is the *absence* of faith! Anything that is not of faith is sin.

If we are not treating our spouse in a godly manner it is because there is an absence of faith – that absence of faith keeps me from going to God through Christ, too. It is only because of Christ that I can come into the presence of God and it is only because of Christ that I can perform a Spiritual action. I cannot perform a "good" deed and somehow qualify for an answer to prayer; that would not be just or fair. God is just; we all have the same opportunity and that opportunity is Jesus Christ. As you go to God in prayer remember that it is only through Christ that you have the right to enter the throne room and it is only through Christ that you can do anything that the Bible instructs you to do.

In Deuteronomy we see another example of how the Word produces Spiritual fruit – how Spirit gives birth to Spirit.

Deuteronomy 17:18-20 (Ampl.) And when he sits on his royal throne, he shall write for himself a copy of this law in a book, out of what is before the Levitical priests. And he shall keep it with him, and he shall read in it all the days of his life, that he may learn [reverently] to fear the Lord his God, by keeping all the words of this law and these statutes and doing them. That his [mind and] heart may not be lifted up above his brethren and that he may not turn aside from the commandment to the right hand or to the left; so that he may continue long, he and his sons, in his kingdom in Israel.

The king was instructed to copy the law for himself; he had to personally copy word-for-word what God had said. He could not pass this task off to another. This written copy was to be read by him every day *in order for him to be able to do what the law had stated.* We notice the words "keeping" and "doing." Keeping, once again, is defined as keeping your eyes on, hedging in as with thorns, or protecting. Keeping leads to doing; abiding in the Word will produce faith and faith will produce Spiritual actions. Turning aside from the law is taking your focus off of the Word. When you turn aside your view changes; you are no longer focusing on the same thing. We can turn aside from the Word and put our focus on the world, our circumstances, others, and so on.

We must recognize that we are breaking faith or being untrue to who we are in Christ when we believe that we can somehow do enough to qualify for answered prayer. Our flesh takes the reins as we attempt to achieve an answer to prayer and the Spirit takes a back seat. The "qualifications" become our focus rather than Jesus Christ. We become more concerned with what we are attempting to do rather than what Christ wants to do through us. People do not have to be told the qualifications for answered prayer; people simply need to be educated on abiding in the Word. The Word of God will produce the faith that will result in the Spiritual actions.

It is no longer necessary to dictate to others what they should or shouldn't do when faith is involved; faith has Spiritual action "attached" to it! Faith, which comes from abiding in the Word, will produce Spiritual actions in you without any other action on your part.

This is hard for some to accept. Working and earning have been ingrained in us since childhood; nonetheless, that is not how things operate in the Spirit.

Seeing the Spiritual value of remaining focused on the Word alone, it would be beneficial for us to promptly recognize what takes our focus off of Christ. Guard your Spirit, and at times you will even have to do so against so-called Spiritual ideas. Any idea that puts the focus on you rather than on God is indeed of the flesh – even if it is taught in the church.

Continuing with the blessings that have been bestowed on us, the final blessing we will look at is the blessing of God's provision. God has promised to supply all of our needs.

Philippians 4:19 (NIV) And my God will meet all your needs according to His glorious riches in Christ Jesus.

This is an awesome promise with vast possibilities; *all* of my needs will be met. Your needs are whatever God has promised you! The word "needs" was translated from a word that means claims, demands, and wants. We cannot demand anything from God if we do not first know what was promised because to demand does not mean to boss God around; it means to claim what is rightfully yours.

Do I act covertly and live wondering how I am going to take care of this or that? Do I live like a mere man with limited resources when the God of this universe is in covenant relationship with me? I am dealing deceitfully with myself and others when I do. There are specific promises for specific needs and I must seek them out. I can only put an end to the charade by putting the Word to work in my life.

We must promptly realize that the Word is the only thing we truly necessitate in this life!

> **Psalms 27:4-5 (NIV) One thing I ask of the LORD, this is what I seek: that I may dwell in the house of the LORD all the days of my life, to gaze upon the beauty of the LORD and to seek Him in His temple. For in the day of trouble He will keep me safe in His dwelling; He will hide me in the shelter of His tabernacle and set me high upon a rock.**

David only asked for *one* thing; that one thing was to be in God's presence – in the Spirit, in the heavenly realms.

Being in God's presence is being in agreement with His Word; we are in agreement because we *abide* in His Word and it produces faith.

David was familiar with the complete care that was provided in God's presence. He knew God would take care of him and keep him safe. David knew the Word would put him in the position he desired to be in; David knew that the life he longed to live could only be found in the Word of God.

In this life we have many choices to make; however, no choice is as important as the one we make in regards to the Word of God. What I choose to do with the Word determines the kind of life I live. Do not forget; broken faith leads to broken lives.

It is time for Christians to drop the "mild-mannered reporter" act and live the super hero life all day, every day! Why should we live below God's best when we can live by faith

Chapter 10
HELP FOR YOUR UNBELIEF

Mark 9:24 (NIV)

Immediately the boy's father exclaimed, "I do believe; help me overcome my unbelief!"

The statement, "I believe; help me overcome my unbelief," signifies a contradiction of thoughts. One thought agrees with the Word of God while the other opposes it. Each thought has an origin; the origin being either the Spirit or the flesh. Our flesh produces thoughts of doubt and our Spirit produces thoughts of faith. We found that the Spirit is strengthened by our intake of the Word of God. Our flesh is strengthened by our intake of all that disagrees with the Word.

We must understand that we have two identities to live with: our Spiritual identity and our identity in the flesh.

2 Corinthians 5:17 (KJV) Therefore if any man [be] in Christ, [he is] a new creature: old things are passed away; behold, all things are become new.

Once we accept Christ as our personal Savior we become a new creation. Old things are "passed away." This does not mean that they are dead, however. The phrase, "passed away," was translated from a word that means to come near or aside. The old man now has something new coming near or coming in alongside of the old and it is referred to as our Spiritual identity.

As a Christian, I must understand that I have two natures. The Holy Spirit in me is my Spiritual nature and my flesh is my carnal nature. The Spiritual nature is in agreement with the things of God and the flesh is enmity with God. I must understand how to yield to the Spirit.

The two natures that we now deal with are enemies. The Spirit hates the things of the flesh and the flesh hates the things of the Spirit. The flesh is our enemy. The flesh hates the things of God. If we want to enjoy our lives and walk in all that God has for us, then we must learn how to walk in the Spirit and ignore the flesh.

Our consistent use of the Word will bring our Spiritual nature to the forefront. We were born again through the Word of God and we must live our lives through the Word of God.

1 Peter 1:23 (NIV) For you have been born again, not of perishable seed, but of imperishable, through the living and enduring Word of God.

We received Christ by grace through faith (Ephesians 2:8). Grace is the Divine influence on our heart in our daily lives; in other words, grace is synonymous with the Word of God. We are influenced daily through the Word. His Word is Spirit and it is life (John 6:63). When we abide in the Word, we are receiving His life and we are taking part in that which is Spiritual.

As we heard the Word of God on salvation, faith was produced and we then received Christ's sacrifice for us. We could not receive Christ without the Word – He is the Word. Only the Word produces Spiritual faith (Romans 10:17). Similarly, we cannot live a Spiritual life without the Word.

Colossians 2:6-7 (NIV) So then, just as you received Christ Jesus as Lord, continue to live in Him, rooted and built up in Him, strengthened in the faith as you were taught, and overflowing with thankfulness.

We must live in the same way that we received Christ – by grace through faith. Our roots must be in Him. Our salvation is based on Him and so is our Spiritual life here on earth. If we decide to find our strength in ourselves, then we are not living by faith – we are living in the flesh.

The Bible tells us that the righteous will live by faith (Galatians 3:11) – those who know who they are in Christ know that they are righteous and they know that they can only live a Spiritual life through Christ (the Word). They know that the Word alone will produce the faith that they require to live a Spiritual life.

Do you depend on the Word to produce faith in your life or are you depending on your efforts?

Walking in the Spirit requires the Word. We must be consistently ingesting the Word, but even when our Spiritual identity is at the forefront, our flesh loves to invade our lives. Doubt creeps in when we least expect it. It can overtake us if we are not careful. The boy's father knew the answer to his doubt; the answer was to call out for help!

Do we call out for help or do we try to handle the doubt ourselves? Do we give doubt the power to make us feel as if we are not successful as a Christian? Do we then, because of the doubt, try to rectify the situation ourselves? *We* cannot produce faith in our lives and we cannot maintain it! The sooner we realize our need for help, the quicker we will go to God for the help that we need.

John 15:16 (KJV) Ye have not chosen Me, but I have chosen you, and ordained you, that ye should go and bring forth fruit, and [that] your fruit should remain: that whatsoever ye shall ask of the Father in My name, He may give it you.

Jesus said that He ordained us to go and bring forth fruit – Spiritual fruit. The word "ordained" means to place or put in a horizontal position, to make passive. This means that our flesh has to be inactive in order for us to operate in the Spirit. A horizontal position signifies sleep or death. We have to put our flesh in a horizontal position by focusing on Christ and letting Him work through us. *I* cannot produce faith; faith has a Spiritual source. I need to let the Word (Jesus Christ) fill me and flow out of me. If I desire Spiritual fruit that will remain for eternity, then I must understand my need for the Word. I am responsible for my intake of the Word.

Admitting our uncertainty and crying out to God for the help that we require is not a negative action. It is opening our eyes to our desperate need for Christ – our continual need! Never underestimate your need for Christ.

Matthew 14:25-33 (NIV) And in the fourth watch [*between 3:00--6:00 a.m.*] of the night, Jesus came to them, walking on the sea.   And when the disciples saw Him walking on the sea, they were terrified and

said, It is a ghost! And they screamed out with fright. But instantly He spoke to them, saying, Take courage! I AM! Stop being afraid! And Peter answered Him, Lord, if it is You, command me to come to You on the water. He said, Come! So Peter got out of the boat and walked on the water, and he came toward Jesus. But when he perceived and felt the strong wind, he was frightened, and as he began to sink, he cried out, Lord, save me [*from death*]! Instantly Jesus reached out His hand and caught and held him, saying to him, O you of little faith, why did you doubt? And when they got into the boat, the wind ceased. And those in the boat knelt and worshiped Him, saying, Truly You are the Son of God!

Peter was not shy when it came to crying out for help. He was not worried about what his friends might think. He was not agonizing over his doubt. He did not believe that his lack of faith would disqualify him from the help that he required. As soon as he began to sink, he cried out. We must do the same. Do not attempt to handle it on your own. We need Christ's help and we need it now! Instantly, Jesus reached out to Peter and He will do the same for us. He is not waiting for us to earn His help. If we could earn it, then we would not really need it.

Jesus asked Peter why he was of "little faith." Little faith is defined as incredulous and lacking confidence in Christ. Peter was skeptical; he was not completely convinced. We see this demonstrated in his words. He said to Jesus, "...*if* it is You." If is not certain; if denotes doubt. His flesh battled with his Spirit as he found himself wanting to step out. His doubt did not kick in after he walked on the water; it was at work before he even put one foot out of the boat. Your flesh will do the same; it will attack before you make a move and it will not die without a fight! Peter stepped out and his doubt kicked in again. Have you experienced times of great faith that enabled you to step out only to find yourself sinking in doubt? Do not feel alone – Peter experienced this. Many times we look at the people in the Bible as "super" Spiritual; when in fact, they are just like you and me. Their examples should motivate us. If you find yourself in doubt at any time, then you need to cry out for help. Allow Jesus to take your hand and remove the doubt.

Jesus asked Peter why he doubted – we do not *have* to doubt, but that does not mean we will *not* doubt. *Why* did he doubt? His perception and his feelings are listed as the reasons. He perceived the storm as a danger. How do we identify the storms in our lives? Jesus did not view the storm as a danger; it did not stop Him from moving forward. If we look at the storm in a Biblical manner, then we will also move ahead with Christ. Perception is the key.

2 Corinthians 4:17-18 (NIV) For our light and momentary troubles are achieving for us an eternal glory that far outweighs them all. So we fix our eyes not on what is seen, but on what is unseen. For what is seen is temporary, but what is unseen is eternal.

Paul perceived his trials as light and momentary. He also viewed them in comparison with what they would accomplish. If we look at our problems in this manner, then we will find ourselves in a place where we can enjoy our lives even though we are going through trials. Paul's perception differed from Peter's. Peter looked at his storm as being dangerous whereas Paul saw his trials as harmless. When we fix our eyes on the promises of God we will be victorious. Focusing on the trial defeats us.

Peter's feelings were the other motivation for his doubt. Our feelings are fickle; they change like the weather. The storms in our lives will cause us to experience a number of different feelings, but we must not allow them to control us. If our feelings begin to produce doubt, then we must cry out to God. Peter felt the pressure of the wind and the waves; you may also feel the pressures that your storms produce. A storm generates wind, waves, thunder, lightening, and the like. Your storm will likewise bring about the potentially dangerous but you can escape if you have shelter. Jesus Christ is our place of protection and we must recognize this.

2 Kings 6:15-17 (NIV) When the servant of the man of God got up and went out early the next morning, an army with horses and chariots had surrounded the city. "Oh, my lord, what shall we do?" the servant asked. "Don't be afraid," the prophet answered. "Those who are with us are more than those who are with them." And Elisha prayed, "O LORD, open his eyes so he may see." Then the LORD opened the servant's eyes, and he looked and saw the hills full of horses and chariots of fire all around Elisha.

Horses and chariots were the potentially dangerous according to Elisha's servant. He saw them clearly with his own two eyes and immediately fear entered the picture. Elisha avoided the fear factor by focusing on the Spiritual. Elisha knew that what he could see physically was no match for the Spiritual, or what he could not physically see. He prayed for his servant's eyes to be opened. He wanted him to also recognize that there was no reason to fear.

We must see our situation in a Spiritual manner. We must look at things the way God looks at them. In Nehemiah, chapter four and verse fourteen, the people had to look at their situation based on the Spiritual. There was an enemy approaching, but they needed to focus on their great and awesome God.

Nehemiah knew that his focus was imperative. *After* he looked things over, things changed; fear was expelled. The fear was removed because he looked at things based on the Spiritual; he saw the situation according to God's promises. He looked at the circumstances and encouraged others to remember the Lord. If we are focusing on the Lord, then we will not fear. This fearlessness enables us to fight; it gives us the ability to fight for our families, to fight for our blessings, and to fight the good fight of faith for whatever God has promised us!

Peter needed to view things in the same way that Jesus did and thus understand that he had nothing to fear; the wind and waves were no match for His Savior in the same way the horses and chariots were no match for the army God supplied. Whatever you are up against, you can be assured that it is no match for God! Run to Him and stand up against your battles through Christ! Quickly proceed to your shelter; your shelter is found in Jesus Christ – and He is the Word! The Word will protect us during these storms; it will keep the potentially dangerous at bay.

The statement, "I believe, help my unbelief," is not a demeaning statement. It is an admission of the fact that this man had two natures. This man had to deal with his flesh. It would rear its ugly head when he least expected it and he did not like it. In acknowledging his weakness he could accept Christ's strength.

2 Corinthians 12:9-10 (NIV) But He said to me, "My grace is sufficient for you, for My power is made perfect in weakness." Therefore I will boast all the more gladly about my weaknesses, so that Christ's power may rest on me. That is why, for Christ's sake, I delight in weaknesses, in insults, in hardships, in persecutions, in difficulties. For when I am weak, then I am strong.

As long as we are trying to muster up the strength and faith that we require on our own, then we will not walk in Spiritual strength or Spiritual faith. Admitting our weakness is not a disadvantage; it is to our benefit! Do you remember when Jesus said it was a blessing to be poor in Spirit (Matthew 5:3)? He was referring to this very thing. The poor in Spirit are those who know that they are Spiritually destitute without Christ. They are blessed because they acknowledge their need and they receive Christ and His provision. Those who feel rich in Spirit do not require Christ; they deem themselves Spiritual without Jesus.

Jesus tells us that His grace is sufficient. Grace, we must keep in mind, is synonymous with the Word of God. His grace is sufficient – the Word is enough! If we will continue to abide in His Word, then we will find the strength that we require to overcome our carnal weakness.

Too many times we believe that we must be strong on our own. We are trying to prove our worth and value as a Christian by flexing our muscles, but anything that we can accomplish on our own is nothing more than filthy rags according to God. Man longs to achieve, but God told us that we can only receive.

Isaiah 7:9 (NIV) …If you do not stand firm in your faith, you will not stand at all.

I used to look at this verse as a challenge. I felt that I had to stand firm and prove my faith until I studied this verse. The phrase "stand firm" comes from one Hebrew word – *aman*. *Aman* is also translated as "believe," "established," and "faithful" in Scripture. This word amazed me. It means to be built up or supported, to be fostered by a parent, and to be nursed by a father. We all know that a father does not nurse a child in the natural – but our Father does just that in the Spirit! If we are not being built up and supported by God, if we are not being fostered by our Father and nursed by our Father, then we will not be able to stand! He fosters, He supports, and He nurses through the Word – by faith. We must receive from Him!

This word *aman* also means to be rendered firm and faithful; this, again, means that *He* makes me faithful. We must remember our only Spiritual source! Apart from Christ we can do nothing of Spiritual value – never forget this!

It seems unnatural to boast about our weakness – actually, it is – it is super-natural! We will boast about our weakness only when we are walking in the Spirit or walking in the strength that Christ provides.

When you are in the process of believing God and you feel doubt creep in, call out to Him! Acknowledge your weakness and receive the strength that only He can provide. Help for our unbelief can only come from Him and He is only a cry away!

Chapter 11
A WORD OF FAITH

Luke 7:1-9 (NIV)
When Jesus had finished saying all
this in the hearing of the people, He entered
Capernaum. There a centurion's servant, whom
his master valued highly, was sick and about to
die. The centurion heard of Jesus and sent some
elders of the Jews to Him, asking Him to come
and heal his servant. When they came to Jesus,
they pleaded earnestly with Him, "This man
deserves to have you do this, because he loves
our nation and has built our synagogue." So
Jesus went with them. He was not far from the
house when the centurion sent friends to say to
Him: "Lord, don't trouble yourself, for I do not
deserve to have You come under my roof. That is
why I did not even consider myself worthy to
come to You. But say the word, and my servant
will be healed. For I myself am a man under
authority, with soldiers under me. I tell this one,
'Go,' and he goes; and that one, 'Come,' and he
comes. I say to my servant, 'Do this,' and he does
it." When Jesus heard this, He was amazed at
him, and turning to the crowd following Him, He
said, "I tell you, I have not found such great faith
even in Israel."

In the Gospels we find a story that has always sparked something in me. I believe the phrase "such great faith" is what captured my attention.

What was so great about this man's faith? What made Jesus designate this man's faith as the greatest even in all of Israel? This man did not need to witness anything with his eyes; he only required a word. Faith is the substance of things hoped for, the evidence of things *unseen*. He only considered it necessary that Jesus speak the word. The greatness or the vastness of his faith was based on its "blindness." The less we can see the greater our faith has to be.

The word "great" means vast. Vast means large or enormous; it is talking about size. Our faith has dimension; this indicates that our faith can grow. Our faith can increase; and in contrast, it can decrease. The Word of God informs us that we have been given a measure of faith.

Romans 12:3 (NIV) For by the grace given me I say to every one of you: Do not think of yourself more highly than you ought, but rather think of yourself with sober judgment, in accordance with the measure of faith God has given you.

A measure of faith has been given to us courtesy of God. We did not earn this faith or somehow do something to deserve it – it was a gift from God. We are reminded to be humble concerning this gift – faith will move mountains, but we must remember the source of our faith and not take credit for the work that faith does in our lives.

God has given each of us a measure of faith. This measure is our responsibility. What are we going to do with it? Are we going to use the Word of God to grow our faith or are we going to ignore the Word and ignore our faith?

> **Mark 4:24-25 (NIV)** **"Consider carefully what you hear," He continued. "With the measure you use, it will be measured to you--and even more. Whoever has will be given more; whoever does not have, even what he has will be taken from him."**

Consider carefully what you hear – faith comes from hearing the Word – be aware of how much of the Word you are taking in. Are you filling yourself with the Word or are you barely getting a snack? The person who fills up on the Word will receive more Spiritually because the Word is our Spiritual Seed – how much fruit you desire is directly related to how much seed you scatter.

The process of growing our faith will be different for each individual, but one thing remains the same – the only seed of faith is the Word.

We cannot have faith without the Word. We develop our faith and instigate its growth when we continue in the Word of God.

The greater the development of our faith, the more apparent it is in our lives. Our words will proclaim our faith, our actions will display our faith, our thoughts will coincide with our faith, and so on.

As we look back to this passage of Scripture in Luke, we find the elders singing the centurion's praises for the work he performed while the centurion modestly admits he does not warrant anything from Jesus – building the synagogue did not secure his right to receive a miracle and he was well aware of that. He even realized that he did not *merit* an audience with the Lord; yet, he did not allow his humility to inhibit his plea. He sent someone else in his place, an intercessor if you will, to make his request. We must understand that we do not warrant an audience with God without our Intercessor, either. We can only go to God through Christ.

This man knew that faith alone was the answer to his problem and he also knew the source of faith – the Word of Christ. He needed a word; we need a word.

Psalms 107:20 (NIV)   He sent forth His word and healed them; He rescued them from the grave.

The Word of God is our deliverance. It rescues us from the grave. The grave, in this particular instance, means a pitfall or any destruction. We can also look at this as referring to death. God sent forth Jesus and healed us. He rescued us from death. For God so loved the world that He sent His only Son that whoever would believe in Him would not perish but would have eternal life (John 3:16). If God did not love us so, then He would not have sent His Son to take our place on the cross and *we* would have had to die for our sins; we would not have the option of deliverance from a place called hell through Christ's sacrifice. Fortunately, we have a God who loves us so much that He did not spare His own Son; *but*, He freely gave Him up for us all (Romans 8:32). In the same way we have to choose to accept Christ as Savior, we have to decide to accept and utilize the Word of God and all that it offers. Faith is available to us; it is not forced on us. He sent forth His Word, but you have to reach out and take hold of it.

He sent forth His Word because there are many pitfalls in this life. The Word of God is what keeps me out of trouble and despair.

Psalms 32:7 (NIV) You are my hiding place; You will protect me from trouble and surround me with songs of deliverance. Selah

The Word of God is my cure for a miserable life! It is my therapy for *whatever* ails me. Jesus gave us His Word – it is our healing. As a Christian, I have the remedy for whatever life throws my way right at my fingertips; I only have to make use of it. He is my hiding place – I can take shelter in His Word while the storm is raging around me because I know that He will take care of me. Victory will be the end result of the storm when Jesus Christ is involved.

We can avoid the additional trouble that trials include when we stay focused on the Word. For example, many times a trial brings along with it the temptation to fear. If I am struggling with fear, then I only need a "word" and Jesus furnished us with a plethora of words regarding fear; furthermore, He did the same for every trouble we may encounter. Whatever the trial includes, I can see victory over it through Christ!

The words that Jesus spoke have power: power to deliver, power to heal, power to set free, and power to do *whatever* needs to be done. The prolific power of His Words will supply you with everything you will ever need.

John 15:7 (KJV) If ye abide in Me, and My words abide in you, ye shall ask what ye will, and it shall be done unto you.

The power of the Word can change our lives, but it is up to us if we use the Word – consider carefully what you are doing with the Word.

Asking and receiving require abiding in Christ. Abiding in Christ is seeing yourself according to who you are in Him. As I go to the Word I must go based on who I am in Christ. I must understand that Christ paid the price for me; He makes me eligible for all of His promises. When I realize this, I then begin to meditate on His promises. I take them in and they become part of who I am. I hold on to the Word because I know I am a rightful heir of all that is Christ's and I begin to boldly go to God for what is rightfully mine.

The Word has power. When Jesus would speak even demons had to listen. There is no power in heaven, under heaven, on earth, under earth, or in hell that is greater than the Word of God.

Luke 4:36 (NIV) All the people were amazed and said to each other, "What is this teaching? With authority and power He gives orders to evil spirits and they come out!"

Matthew 8:16-17 (NIV) When evening came, many who were demon-possessed were brought to Him, and He drove out the spirits with a word and healed

all the sick. This was to fulfill what was spoken through the prophet Isaiah: "He took up our infirmities and carried our diseases."

The demon-possessed were set free *with a word*! The power in the words of Christ is unrivaled! He is the Word! There is no power that is greater than the Word of God and this Word has been entrusted to us! We have this Word readily available to us. Demons cannot stand against it and neither can our problems!

The power that is in the Word of God is indescribable. There is no power that it can be compared to. Jesus would speak the word and disease would have to leave the body it inhabited without delay (Luke 4:39; 5:13). No sickness or disease could stand against Jesus Christ and His Word. We have the ability to come against whatever is attacking us in the name of Jesus according to the Word of God.

John 14:12 (NIV) I tell you the truth, anyone who has faith in Me will do what I have been doing. He will do even greater things than these, because I am going to the Father.

Faith manifests the Word in our lives; faith is the producer of all Spiritual actions. Our faith is in Him – we know that He can do anything and that He will work through us. We know that all of His promises are sure. We do not have to fear anything when we know the Word of God. **Faith alleviates fear.**

The Word declares that He took up our infirmities and carried our diseases, past tense. My healing (in every area) has *already* been purchased by the blood of Christ. A lack of faith is only postponing the delivery. We have been given the Word to provide us with what we require to cultivate our faith; apply it! Read the Word, meditate on the Word, memorize the Word, and speak the Word.

As we begin to feed on the Word, we will also experience change in our words. We will speak the Word when our hearts of full of the Word. Our words can speak life or death – they will speak life when we are full of the Word.

Numbers 14:28 (NIV) So tell them, "As surely as I live, declares the LORD, I will do to you the very things I heard you say."

The creative power of our words does not have to be a scary proposition. This declaration by God should prompt us to diligence in regards to storing the Word of God in our hearts to ensure the Spiritual origin of the words proceeding from our mouth. When the words of our mouth are in agreement with the Word of God we can anticipate the fulfillment of God's promises – and that is an exciting proposition!

God calls those things which be not as though they are (Romans 4:17); He commands the watery deep to become dry (Isaiah 44:27). This signifies that the impossible is possible *when* God is involved. As mentioned, when you discover more and more of the promises in the Word of God you will find that many of them *appear* impossible, but you must remember that God can do the impossible! The word "impossible" is not in God's vocabulary; He calls those things that be not as though they are!

Death becomes life when the Word is involved (Luke 8:52-55). Jesus can speak life into your dead situation. We must realize the transforming power that is in the Word of God. We need to recognize what we have possession of in the Word of God. God blesses us with His words. If He declared it, then we can receive it!

Proverbs 3:33 (Ampl.)   ...He declared blessed (joyful and favored with blessings) the home of the righteous!

God blesses us simply by saying, by declaring, by speaking! His Word is our blessing! The more we are focused on the Word the more our faith grows, and the more our faith grows the more we see the promises in His Word come to pass in our lives.

It is all about faith that works by His love for us. Some people insinuate that faith alone is insufficient; however, they are incorrect. People attempt to rationalize the need to add something to our faith. They argue that they are right because they observe people *saying* they believe God and yet a number of those same people never experience the promises; however, **simply saying that you believe something is not proof of faith.** Furthermore, they do not understand the difference between living faith and dead faith. Dead faith can talk all day long, but it will never produce Spiritual fruit. When God says faith and patience inherit the promises that is what He means! We do not have to add to the Word. We do not have to try to explain God. He explains Himself perfectly; we simply need to study what He has truly said.

As we discussed, faith without works is dead; consequently, we have concluded that there is also living faith that *will* produce works. We also know that the Spirit gives life; therefore, anything living is of the Spirit! Spiritual faith is alive; it produces fruit; it brings promises to pass in our lives. A person who has Spiritual faith will have the Word to back them up and they *will* see the promise come to pass in their life in God's perfect timing.

Great faith should be our goal and great faith will only be produced by abiding in the Word. His Word is our blessing. Our attention to the Word makes our faith great and it changes our lives!

Chapter 12
FAITH SPEAKS

Luke 6:45 (NIV)
The good man brings good things out of the good stored up in his heart, and the evil man brings evil things out of the evil stored up in his heart. For out of the overflow of his heart his mouth speaks.

As we continue on our journey to understand what faith encompasses, it is essential to remember that faith is Spiritual (meaning that its source is the Word of God); therefore, we cannot have faith outside of the Word of God. Our claim to believe God lies dormant if we lack the endorsement of Scripture. Many times we *assume* that we believe God when, in fact, our actions and our words demonstrate otherwise. To be truly in faith, one's actions, thoughts, and words must collectively line up in agreement – and this only comes to pass as we consistently abide in the Word of God. Our heart is the source of our words and sin is avoided by retaining the Word in our heart (Psalm 119:11).

In this chapter we will discuss the ways in which faith affects our words, how it alters the very language we speak, and we will also discover how these new words of faith produce life (or something Spiritual) in our lives.

The good man brings good out of the good that is stored in his heart. Who is the good man? The good man is the Spiritual man. Only God is good (Mark 10:18) – and we are good when we are walking in His Spirit. When we walk in the Spirit we will not speak against the Word of God; our words will agree with His because they will be His! When our hearts are full of the Word of God, then our words will be good or they will be Spiritual. Conversely, evil is spoken when evil is what fills the heart.

A person who lives by faith has a vocabulary unlike most. While others are proclaiming pessimism and fearfulness, confidence and courage pour forth from the mouths of the faith-filled. The person of faith is intimate with the Word and they are personally acquainted with God's promises; the Word of God is their dwelling place and it is unmistakable in their speech. Words of faith can only be verbalized as the result of storing up the Word of God in our hearts; so once again, we see the invaluable impact of the Word of God and its product of faith in our lives.

Knowing that we require the Word in our hearts we may ask ourselves, "How can I store the Word in my heart?"

Psalms 45:1 (NIV) My heart is stirred by a noble theme as I recite my verses for the king; my tongue is the pen of a skillful writer.

Proverbs 7:3 (NIV) Bind them on your fingers; write them on the tablet of your heart.

Reading is the obvious way to store the Word of God inside your heart, but in Psalms and Proverbs we see another way – another way that is connected with faith. In the Psalms the Psalmist refers to his tongue as a pen and he signifies that he is reciting his verses; he is speaking the Word out loud. In Proverbs we find that the Word needs to be written on our heart. Obviously, it is not physically possible to write on our heart. As we read the verses above, we can conclude that our vocalization of the Word of God inscribes it on our heart; furthermore, we recall that faith, as well, is the end result of hearing the Word. Verbalizing the Word is far more beneficial than we may realize. Speak the Word, sing the Word, shout the Word, and do so every chance you get!

The significance of faith and the Word in our everyday communications is of primary importance. Faith talks and it speaks the Word, but on the other hand, doubt and unbelief speak destruction.

Proverbs 15:4 (NIV) The tongue that brings healing is a tree of life, but a deceitful tongue crushes the spirit.

A deceitful tongue is not simply referring to a person who does not tell the facts of the matter. The meaning of this verse is diluted if we look at it that way. True a deceitful tongue belongs to the person who does not speak the truth, but what truth is being referred to? The Word of God is truth; therefore, the person with a deceitful tongue is the person who speaks in contrast to the Word of God. When our words are contrary to the Word of God we crush our Spirit. Our Spirit is built up by the Word of God and we necessitate a strong Spirit if we yearn to withstand this fight of faith. We are ensuring defeat by speaking deceitfully and, as a consequence, crushing our Spirit.

Proverbs 13: 3 (NIV) He who guards his lips guards his life, but he who speaks rashly will come to ruin.

Speaking rashly or allowing your mouth to function without the Word of God leads to ruin. All of us have our moments when we say things we regret; we need the "mouth filter" that the Word of God provides from the heart. Guarding our lips can only be done through God; it is not something we will accomplish on our own.

Apart from Christ we cannot accomplish anything Spiritual and this cannot be communicated too many times or in too many ways!

The Bible tells us that no man can tame the tongue (James 3:8); nonetheless, it encouragingly informs that what is impossible for *man* is possible for *God* (Matthew 19:26).

Psalms 141:3 (NIV) Set a guard over my mouth, O LORD; keep watch over the door of my lips.

During this fight of faith our words can make or break us, but we must keep in mind that the words that will bring us victory have their source in the Word of God alone. The guard that will be set over our mouth is placed at the door of our lips, which is our heart. The guard is the accumulation of the Word of God in our hearts. As you read ask God to store the Word inside of you; claim retention. Speak the Word out loud and sing songs full of the Word.

A clear indicator of your level of faith is your words. If your words do not compliment those things you assume you believe, then you must "stock up!" A shortage of faith-filled words is due to a lack of the Word, and that is easily rectified. If you are deficient in the Word of God, then your vocabulary will give you away; on the other hand, out of the overflow of the Word in your heart your mouth will bless you.

Proverbs informs us of the benefits of a mouth that is full of the Word of God (Proverbs 12:14). Faith-filled words will fill us with good things. We must recognize the impact that our words have on our lives.

> **James 3:3-5 (ESV) If we put bits into the mouths of horses so that they obey us, we guide their whole bodies as well. Look at the ships also: though they are so large and are driven by strong winds, they are guided by a very small rudder wherever the will of the pilot directs. So also the tongue is a small member.**

Many times we underestimate our words and their power. In the same way a large ship is guided and directed by a comparatively small rudder, the course of my life is determined by the words of my mouth which seem, in comparison, small. The pilot or captain controls the rudder; I control what goes into my heart which in turn will come out of my mouth. If I am living a life that is dissatisfying I need to examine my intake. What am I filling myself with? What words are coming out of my mouth? A negative person is filled with negative thoughts; therefore, that person speaks negatively. God directs us to speak according to what we long to see; negative speaking indicates a desire for the negative. Most people would disagree with this and argue that they are only speaking the truth, but what truth are they speaking exactly? It is the "truth" of *the world* that is negative; the truth of the Word of God is positive. I am not suggesting that we live blind to the pessimistic circumstances that surround us, but I am saying that we must choose to focus on the truth of God's Word rather than on those circumstances. We must focus on the unseen, not that which can be seen.

As we believe God for His promises, we may look at others who have less and who are in desperate situations and we may feel guilty asking for more. God does not want you to feel guilty; He wants you to be inspired to teach *them* how *they* can have more, too. God's promises are not just for a select group; they are for "whosoever will!" If we would all get in agreement with God's promised blessings, then what an impact we would have on the world; after all, God does want to bless us in order for us to be a blessing.

You may be in a very desperate situation right now but God declares that circumstances do not limit Him; nothing is impossible with Him! Instead of declaring what is wrong, you must declare the Word.

Previously, we discussed magnifying the Lord instead of our problems. To magnify the Word or the Lord means to make it the principal passion in our lives.

Isaiah 42:21 (KJV) The LORD is well pleased for His righteousness' sake; He will magnify the law, and make [it] honorable.

God magnifies His Word and we should do the same. He has declared the "enormity" of His Word; it is chief; it is to be magnified.

We magnify the Word when we verbalize it as a replacement for the negative words we could be speaking. How "big" is the Word in your life? In answering this question you must be honest with yourself. If your words are words of negativity, then you do not need to be hard on yourself or feel guilty – you simply must realize that you necessitate more of the Word of God in your heart. The Word is the answer to your problem of negative speaking. This quandary of negative speaking is more correctly defined as a crisis. Our words are a life altering force in our lives and we must fully appreciate this.

As we ponder the life-changing power our words have it is important for us to recall that words of faith will produce Spiritual fruit!

Isaiah 44:24-27 (NIV) "This is what the LORD says-- your Redeemer, who formed you in the womb: I am the LORD, who has made all things...who carries out the words of His servants and fulfills the predictions of His messengers...who says to the watery deep, 'Be dry, and I will dry up your streams...'"

Numbers 14:28 (NIV) So tell them, "As surely as I live, declares the LORD, I will do to you the very things I heard you say."

I find these verses to be amazing; for that reason, they bear repeating. God is telling us that He will carry out the words of His servants; astounding. His servants or His messengers are speaking IIis Word – that is why He guarantees fulfillment.

Do we really perceive what is being articulated by God? God is telling us that our words are particularly vital; they have intrinsic value. He is telling us that our words have creative power; they determine our life.

Proverbs 18:21 (NIV) The tongue has the power of life and death, and those who love it will eat its fruit.

Our words have the power to create life (something Spiritual) or death (something of the flesh). Do we love our flesh? Do we love it to the point that our heart is overflowing with it and the words that are coming out of our mouth agree with it instead of the Word of God? If we do, then we need to be prepared to eat the fruit of the flesh. If you read Galatians chapter five, verses twenty-two through twenty-three, you will find the fruit of the Spirit; the fruit of the flesh is the other extreme. Are you prepared to eat hatred, unhappiness, and anxiety, to name just a few? If an arduous life is not the life you want for yourself, then you must understand the power of your words and their source.

You may think, "What is she thinking? Do I love my flesh? What kind of question is that? Of course, I do not love my flesh! I just cannot help myself! This is too hard!" Your feelings are valid, yet they must not be permitted to dominate you. You may feel as if it is easier said than done to read, but you have need of it nevertheless. A person who requires kidney dialysis may find that it is difficult to go for treatment day after day, but they go if they value life. This fight we are in cannot be fought by our feelings. Slogans such as, "Pain is weakness leaving the body," and "If you are ready to quit them I am ready to finish you off," are boldly plastered on t-shirts and athletes proudly dress in them; I think Christians should clothe themselves mentally with such apparel. We need to be of the mindset that dying to our flesh might be painful but it is a pain that is facilitating the removal of our flesh and all of its weakness; therefore, it is worth it. Weakness is leaving our body when our flesh cries out in pain. Jesus suffered in the garden as His flesh did battle with His Spirit; He did so to the point that He sweat drops of blood. He was a man and He was the Son of God in the same way that we are Spirit and flesh. Certainly He was without sin and we are still subject to the frustration of our sin (Romans 8:20), but in order for us to reign with Him we also have to suffer with Him (Philippians 3:10) – and the battle between your Spirit and your flesh is the suffering being referred to. It is not some twisted form of suffering such as disease, poverty, anger, addictions, hopelessness, and the like.

It will not always be simple to fight for your faith, it will not always be easy to store up the Word in your heart, but it will be effortless to reap the fruit that faith and faith-filled words bring into being. Seeing that we continue to have a flesh to deal with, we must understand that we will have our moments of suffering due to that flesh. We will encounter times of suffering when our faith is put to the test. At different times in life each of us will have our faith tested and at that time our mouth needs to be prepared – this means that our hearts must be full of the Word!

Romans 8:28, 31-32 (KJV) And we know that all things work together for good to them that love God,

to them who are the called according to [His] purpose…What shall we then *say* to these things? If God [be] for us, who [can be] against us? He that spared not His own Son, but delivered Him up for us all, how shall He not with Him also freely give us all things?

In Romans we find an interesting phrase, "What shall we *say* to these *things*?" What shall we *say* to the things that are taking place in our life that we do not take pleasure in? I realize most people would think only an insane person would talk to things or situations, but here in the Word of God we are instructed to do exactly that. We will benefit from having a discussion with these situations. We need to speak the truth of the Word of God. We need to voice the certainty that God will work this situation out for our good; we need to repeatedly state that God is working on our behalf no matter what our situation may display. It is crucial for us to recognize that the circumstances in life are declaring something and we must say something in response, immediately!

Faith that is alive will speak; it cannot remain silent. Faith commands the situations in your life to line up with the Word of God. Faith is not afraid to voice what is impossible for man.

Matthew 21:21(NIV) Jesus replied, "I tell you the truth, if you have faith and do not doubt, not only can you do what was done to the fig tree, but also you can *say* to this mountain, 'Go, throw yourself into the sea,' and it will be done."

What "mountain" is standing in your way? Whatever mountain it may be, faith can remove it. The more we are in the Word of God and the more the Word is in us, the more we understand the unlimited power of God. Fear is no longer an issue as we boldly move forward proclaiming the Word of God.

As we continue to study the creative power of words I would like to draw your attention back to the verse in Isaiah, specifically to the phrase, "who says to the watery deep, 'Be dry, and I will dry up your streams.'" Once again we find God telling us that the impossible is possible. The watery deep can be made completely dry when His hand is commissioned. We also saw in Romans that God quickens the dead; He grants or gives life to that which is dead. Is your marriage lifeless? He knows how to bring life to it. Is your relationship with your child indifferent? He can give it vitality. Are your finances comatose? He is able to resurrect them. Is your attitude spent? He can revive it. Whatever is in a state of death in your life can be brought to life when you invite God into the situation! Open the Word of God and discover what His Word declares about your predicament. God calls those things that "be not as though they were." He calls "the watery deep dry" and He wants us to do the same. Call your debt profit! Call your illness a healing! Call your fear faith! Call your failure success! Call your anger self-control! Call your low self-esteem confidence! Call it out in Jesus' name; quote Isaiah and declare that God will carry out your words *according to His promises*!

It is imperative that I continually clarify that only the Word of God produces words in you that will produce life in your situation. Your words must be His words.

John 15:7 (NIV) If you remain in Me and My words remain in you, ask whatever you wish, and it will be given you.

This is not a "name it, claim it" philosophy; this is a Biblical principal. God's word informs us to *ask*; ask in the original language is defined as call out, desire, and require what is rightfully yours. Asking is done with boldness and a person only possesses boldness as a result of *knowing* what is rightfully theirs in Christ. We are told to remain in Christ and let His words remain in us. Remaining in Christ is remaining in your Spiritual identity; it is seeing yourself the way God sees you – in Christ. A deficiency of the Word keeps us ignorant as to what is ours and thereby produces timidity. The Word of

God articulates the inheritance of the Christian; it is the "will" so to speak. If we are to call out for what is ours, then we must be aware of what is ours. I need Biblical proof for what I am calling out for; the Word must remain in me.

The more time you spend in the Word the more you will understand the difference between the Spirit and the flesh; as a result, you will embark on walking more in the Spirit and less in the flesh. Words of faith will increase and words of the flesh will decrease. As your words of faith are amplified you will notice many other positive changes as well. Our words, because of the faith behind them, are a life-giving force.

Proverbs 10:11 (NIV) The mouth of the righteous is a fountain of life, but violence overwhelms the mouth of the wicked.

Our mouths are described as a fountain of life. What a beautiful depiction! The mouth of the righteous, the mouth of the person in Christ, is a flowing, never-ending, supply of life! Provided that I am walking in the Spirit, my mouth is lively and merry. I have a spring in my words and I am giving life to those who listen. Wisdom is found on my lips in view of the fact that the Word is stored up inside of me. I am not giving *my* opinion to others; I am giving them the Word and nothing has more life than the Word. *Our* opinions, even when they line up with the Word, many times contain attitudes of our flesh. For instance, an issue may be clearly defined as wrong in God's Word but we can take that issue and have personal feelings regarding it and our words concerning that issue can then contain death. An issue can be wrong, but Jesus Himself said, "Father, forgive them, for they know not what they are doing."

Preaching or teaching against any particular sin never benefits the listener. In fact, many times, it pushes listeners away, especially the listener who is or has been involved in that sin. When the Pharisees brought Jesus the woman caught in adultery and wanted Him to condemn her, He asked them if they were without sin (John 8:3-7).

We must understand something: the Bible tells us that if we have broken one law we are guilty of breaking every law; therefore, we are *all* equally guilty of *everything*. As we preach against certain sins, in reality, we are preaching against ourselves – even if we may be too blind to realize it.

Sin is a problem, no doubt, but it is *all* sin that is a problem. The sins of doubt, fear, gossip, gluttony, and looking at a woman with lustful thoughts are just as evil as murder, adultery, and rape.

The answer to sin, every single sin, is the Word of God. Instead of preaching on certain sins we need to preach on the life changing power of the Word; the Word has the power to keep us out of sin, every sin – words of condemnation, on the other hand, do not!

Those who walk in the flesh are not enjoying the fruit of their lips. We must realize that we can be walking in our flesh when we are preaching against certain sins. Our flesh becomes puffed up as we preach on something we are not *physically* involved in. We mislead ourselves into believing we are not guilty of these sins, even though the Word tells us otherwise. At what time our flesh is inflated, the Spirit is grieved. Our words are not magnifying God; they are magnifying ourselves and we are using the Word of God to do it. Each of us should praise and thank God for the sins that we are not physically involved in and thank Him for *all* that He has forgiven us for. We must realize where we could be had God not intervened in our lives. Every one of us should stop and meditate on who we could have been were it not for the grace of God. We could be the girl we condemn and tell others about or the guy we avoid at work or on the street. Our words contain power; power to draw people to Christ or push them away from Him. If you were unsaved and you had to listen to someone who spoke exactly like you do, would you want what Jesus had to offer?

God provides us with everything we need to fight our flesh and walk in His Spirit because He knows what the flesh has to offer; He understands the pain and the hurt our flesh produces. Since He is a God who gives us a free-will, He will not force His Word on us; He gives us a choice.

> **Deuteronomy 30:19-20 (NIV) This day I call heaven and earth as witnesses against you that I have set before you life and death, blessings and curses. Now choose life, so that you and your children may live and that you may love the LORD your God, listen to His voice, and hold fast to Him. For the LORD is your life…**

He has left us with the choice of life or death, the Word or our flesh. If we choose life, or the Word (Jesus Christ – John 1:1), then we will live, our children will live, we will love God, we will listen to His voice, and we will hold fast to Him. If we choose our flesh, or death, then we will merely exist. Our lives will be futile and our children will most likely follow in our footsteps; we will not love God, we will not listen to His voice, and we will not hold fast to Him. It is of the utmost importance for us to grasp that the Word of God is the solitary source of Spiritual life. The Word is our means for finding out that God loves us which in turn enables us to love Him, it is the only way to listen to His voice, and it is the only way for us to hold fast to Him. The Word is not simply a book; it is alive and it imparts that Spiritual life to us.

If we want to speak words of life, then we must be full of the Word of God – life itself!

Chapter 13
FAITH-FULL

1 Corinthians 4:2 (NIV)
Now it is required that those who
have been given a trust must prove faithful.

As our study of faith has progressed we have been repeatedly reminded of the fact that we are not responsible for the Spiritual works that faith (God's Word) produces in us. I would like to point out that being faithful is not something we produce in our flesh either.

Reading a verse like the one above makes some feel like they have to achieve a level of faithfulness or they have to make themselves trustworthy. Looking closer at the English word "faithful" should give us a hint that this is not the case. The root word of faithful is "faith;" the suffix "–ful" denotes being full of. We should not misinterpret faithful as trustworthy; being faithful is being full of faith, or in other words, full of the Word!

The Hebrew word *aman* is translated as faithful in many different places and it confirms that faithfulness is from God. Previously, in chapter ten, we saw that this word means to be built up or supported, to be fostered by a parent, to be nursed by a father and to rendered (or made) faithful. This word describes what God does for us – not what we do for God. When we look at the word "faithful" we must not misunderstand its meaning – being faithful is based on receiving from Christ.

We must receive from God; we must be supported by Him! We must receive the Word of God as our Spiritual food and let Him nurse us. As we receive from God we mature Spiritually and we begin to progressively walk in the fruit of the Spirit. We display His qualities as we receive His support and care.

God used the Hebrew word *aman* to describe men such as Abraham, Moses, and David (Nehemiah 9:8; Numbers 12:7; 1 Samuel 22:14) – men who depended on God and walked by faith. God is not expecting us to impress Him with our abilities – He is expecting us to recognize that we cannot impress Him. He is expecting us to recognize our desperate need for Him.

We must always remember that faith that comes from our consistent intake of the Word is the only means of producing Spiritual fruit. If we are filling ourselves with the Word, then we are "faith-full" – and being "faith-full" will, of course, produce Spiritual actions in us. One of those actions that faith produces is dependability, but do not put the cart before the horse. We, on our own, are not dependable; it is Christ in us that will produce steadfastness in our lives.

We must keep the fact that *apart from Christ we can do nothing* in the forefront of our minds at all times. If we begin to imagine that we can somehow prove ourselves faithful enough to deserve something from God, then we are only putting the spotlight on ourselves thus taking it off of Christ. Living by works keeps the focus on man.

The spotlight is on far too many people and it is not focused on Christ nearly enough! *He* must be lifted up if we are going to win others to Him.

Ezekiel 28:2 (NIV) Son of man, say to the ruler of Tyre, this is what the Sovereign LORD says: "In the pride of your heart you say, 'I am a god; I sit on the throne of a god in the heart of the seas.' But you are a man and not a god, though you think you are as wise as a god."

Seeing a verse such as the one above rarely seems to remind us of ourselves. We may think of others or we may think of Satan who wanted to ascend his throne above God's, but we would never think of ourselves. We forget about what we do when we try to accomplish *His* work in our life. Faith, we have found, is a Spiritual gift from a Spiritual source; if we attempt to produce the faith, without the Spiritual source, then we are positioning ourselves in a place above God.

This may sound harsh but it is true, nonetheless. When we try to do something for God instead of allowing God to work through us, we are placing ourselves above Him. We are ignoring our need for Him because we are too focused on self. When we believe that we can achieve on our own apart from Him, we are depending on self rather than God.

We must quickly recognize our position in relation to Christ and the Spiritual things that we need.

2 Corinthians 3:4-6 (NIV) Such confidence as this is ours through Christ before God. Not that we are competent in ourselves to claim anything for ourselves, but our competence comes from God. He has made us competent as ministers of a new covenant--not of the letter but of the Spirit; for the letter kills, but the Spirit gives life.

Faith is produced in my life only because of Christ in me! He has given me of His Holy Spirit and that Spirit imparts life to me through the Word of God. I am not competent in and of myself – my confidence cannot be in what I can do.

Living by the letter, or the law, puts the focus on man's competence. Man erroneously believes that they can be good enough, that they can meet God's requirements. Man cannot live up to the requirements of the law; if we think that we can, then we are deceived. We may appear to be the most dependable and loyal person around, but God is not judging by mere appearances – and neither should we.

The letter kills – it can only produce death or carnal fruit; however, the Spirit gives life. Through Christ I can produce Spiritual fruit – on my own I can only produce works of the flesh that have no Spiritual value. I can only live a Spiritual life through Him. My competence comes from Him – my confidence is in Him alone!

Many will argue that if we love God, then we will do what He says in His Word. There are verses that even seem to agree with this perception; but again, we must always remember one thing – apart from Christ we can do nothing of Spiritual value! We cannot produce one speck of Spiritual action apart from Him! We are dependent on Him.

We must also clearly understand that our love for God does not find its source in us. We can only love Him because He first loved us – His love is the source of our love.

We are told what love is – it is God's love for us, not our love for God (1 John 4:10).

We love Him because He first loved us (1 John 4:19). When we do what God's Word instructs, it is because He loves us – it is not because we love Him! His love is the origination of our Spiritual fruit.

We must keep first things first. We must not forget that! If we will remember that, then we will understand that we can only love Him because He first loved us and we will also understand that any Spiritual fruit that we produce finds its origins in His love for us. We will then be thankful when the Word is manifested in our lives instead of being pompous.

We will never give Him the glory that He deserves if we believe that we are responsible for the "good" things that we do. We will actually expect Him to repay us because we deserve a reward. This kind of thinking is wrong and it will only lead us to a life lived in the flesh.

I cannot misappropriate the recognition for being faithful; the glory goes to God and God alone.

2 Timothy 2:13 (NIV) If we are faithless, He will remain faithful, for He cannot disown himself.

2 Timothy 2:13 (KJV) If we believe not, [yet] He abideth faithful: He cannot deny himself.

God will not deny Himself; the word "deny" means to contradict. He is not relying on me to have enough faith on my own to bring His promises to pass. He knows that I am Spiritually helpless apart from Him (Psalm 103:14) – I need to be sure of this, also. I need to recognize my desperate need for Christ.

Whenever we read the Word and feel as if the burden is on us, we must then dig deeper. God will never leave man with the burden of producing Spiritual fruit because He knows that we are incapable apart from Him – unfortunately, some believe that they are able on their own.

God's Word is not based on man because God knows that we are not capable of bearing such a weight.

Romans 3:3-4a (NIV) What if some did not have faith? Will their lack of faith nullify God's faithfulness? Not at all! Let God be true, and every man a liar.

Praise God! His promises are based on *His* righteousness (Nehemiah 9:8)!

"Let God be true and every man a liar." Before we were in Christ we were simply man. Now that we are in Christ we are not merely flesh, but we now have His Holy Spirit as well. Thanks be to God for bringing us to life Spiritually through Christ and making us competent! We now know how to walk by faith. We possess the ability to be in agreement with God and refrain from the lies.

Matthew 25:21 (NIV) **"His master replied, 'Well done, good and faithful servant! You have been faithful with a few things; I will put you in charge of many things. Come and share your master's happiness!'"**

Jesus refers to the servant as "good and faithful." How can I be a good and faithful servant? I must understand that I am only good because of who I am in Christ.

We must not look at designations such as "good and faithful" and believe that we have to do something to achieve such a title. We are good because Christ is in us and we can be faithful because of what Jesus Christ has freely given us in His Word.

When we understand who we are in Christ and what we have because of Him, then we can share in His joy!

What made this servant faithful? His faithfulness was based on using what his master gave him. He received! If we use what the Master has given us, His Word, then we will find ourselves faithful – full of faith! As we receive nurturing and support from the Word of God we will find that it will produce a harvest of Spiritual fruit in our lives.

We studied the parable of the seed and the sower and we found that the person who has will be given more; this faithful servant had talents and he was blessed with more because he used those talents. If we will use the Word, then we will be amazed at what will be produced in our lives! We have already listed the miraculous results of faith: Spiritual fruit, avoidance of sin, promises fulfilled and much more. Why would we not want to receive from the Word?

A harvest like this brings joy; we enter into our Master's happiness when we are nursed by our loving Father! Jesus told us that His Word makes our joy complete; we need to live accordingly.

John 17:13 (Ampl.) And now I am coming to You; I say these things while I am still in the world, so that My joy may be made full and complete and perfect in them [that they may experience My delight fulfilled in them, that My enjoyment may be

perfected in their own souls, that they may have My gladness within them, filling their hearts].

The words of Jesus Christ are given to us so that we can be full of His joy. Do you understand the benefits of the Word? Do you realize that you are Spiritually bankrupt without the Word? As we understand the value of the Word in our lives we will increasingly abide in it and receive from it and we will become "faith-full" – and He will get all the glory!

Chapter 14
SELF-LESS FAITH

Romans 12:3 (KJV)

For I say, through the grace given unto me, to every man that is among you, not to think [of himself] more highly than he ought to think; but to think soberly, according as God hath dealt to every man the measure of faith.

As we bring this book to a close it is important for us to reiterate how "self-less" faith is. Faith, we have found, is a gift from God; its source is the Word and it is maintained through the Word. Faith is not something that *we* can take credit for. It is not a decision that we make. The amount of faith that we possess is not something *we* can gloat over.

Faith is a gift and we must not identify it as anything other than a gift. We cannot take credit for faith and put ourselves on a pedestal. It is a gift for us to be able to go to the Word for the faith that we require to make it through this life. We cannot depend on ourselves.

2 Corinthians 3:5 (KJV) Not that we are sufficient of ourselves to think anything as of ourselves; but our sufficiency [is] of God.

1 Corinthians 15:10 (KJV) But by the grace of God I am what I am...

I cannot emphasize enough how valuable humility is. Humility is recognizing who you are because of Jesus Christ. Humility is confidence in Christ, not ourselves. When we rely on the Word (Christ) completely then we know that we understand humility. If we are counting on our works, our efforts, our devotion, and the like, then we do not understand humility. True humility keeps you focused on the Word of God because you understand without a doubt that apart from Christ you can do nothing of Spiritual value. The person who is truly humble realizes that nothing good lives in their flesh; they appreciate that they need to be focused on the Word so that they can walk in the Spirit and produce something good, something of eternal value.

As our attention is (progressively) directed toward the Word of God we have found that faith is produced. It is not produced because *we* are superior Christian people; we begin to live by faith because we understand the value of the Word of God. We appreciate the value of breathing; yet, we cannot take credit for the gift of life. We can extinguish the gift of life by refusing to breathe; likewise, we can extinguish the gift of faith by refusing to read the Word. Utilizing the Word is not means for us to sing our own praises; it is reason for us to praise the Lord!

God has bestowed upon each of us a measure of faith; this refers to a limited amount. This amount of faith is limited by us. We limit the faith that is working in our lives by limiting the amount of the Word we take in.

> **Mark 4:24-25 (NKJV) Then He said to them, "Take heed what you hear. With the same measure you use, it will be measured to you; and to you who hear, more will be given. For whoever has, to him more will be given; but whoever does not have, even what he has will be taken away from him."**

To take heed means to look at, to beware, or to perceive. In regards to the Word, are you aware of what you are taking in? Are you concerned with the amount of your intake? We should be.

If I feel a lack of faith in my life, then I can be sure that I am lacking the Word; faith and the Word are in direct relation to each other. More Word equals more faith.

We can also expect God to give liberally and generously; He promises He will give us more than we have taken in. To the person who has the Word more faith will be given, but to the person who lacks the Word the faith he does have will be taken away. This Biblical precept is of significant proportion. It is part of the seed and sower parable and Jesus told us that in understanding this parable we find discernment for the remaining parables. Our comprehensive understanding of faith is fundamental. If we do not understand what His Word truly is, then we will never live the *Zoë* life that He has planned for us.

God wants us to understand the preeminence of His Word in our lives! In doing so, we begin to experience the life that God has for us. The focus needs to be taken off of us if we are going to live by faith. "Self-less" faith is the perfect articulation; it draws attention to the insignificance of our efforts. Faith is selfless because faith is not the end result of us, but of the Word of God!

Too many times the attention is drawn to man. I have heard people say, "I don't know how people who say they are Christians can do some of the things they do," and it makes me cringe. It clearly shows our lack of understanding. Christians can do some of the ungodly things that they do because they still retain a flesh and they are yielding to it. It is not a mystery. We are *all* capable of producing unspiritual fruit. We must understand that the more we abide in disregard for the Word the more we are giving our flesh an invitation to reign.

> **2 Samuel 12:9 (Ampl.) Why have you DESPISED THE COMMANDMENT OF THE LORD, doing evil in His sight? You have slain Uriah the Hittite with the sword and have taken his wife to be your wife. You have murdered him with the sword of the Ammonites.**

To despise the Word of God means to look down on it or disesteem the Word. It also means to view or treat with contempt or disrespect. How do you view the Word? Is it your priority or do you look down on it as something to fill in your spare time? Do you take the Bible with you to church, but leave it on a shelf the rest of the week? Do you read the Word only when you are in trouble? Your answers to questions such as these will open your eyes to how you esteem the Word.

We must also remember that the Word is our weapon against sin – we cannot avoid sin without the Word. When we disesteem the Word of God we *will* do evil in His sight (whether it is doing good in someone else's sight or not!).

> **Proverbs 13:13a (Ampl.)   Whoever despises the Word and counsel [of God] brings destruction upon himself.**

The phrase "brings destruction upon himself" was translated from one Hebrew word – *chabal*. This word means to wind tightly; to bind; to pervert, destroy; to writhe in pain (especially of parturition – the act of giving birth); spoil; travail. Despising the Word will ruin your life – it will pervert your life, it will cause you pain thanks to the fruit your flesh produces, and it will never give you rest.

Psalms 51:4 (KJV) *Against thee, thee only*, **have I sinned, and done [this] evil in Thy sight: that Thou mightest be justified when thou speakest, [and] be clear when Thou judgest.**

Psalm 51 is the Psalm David wrote after Nathan came to him on the subject of Bathsheba. The phrase "against Thee, Thee only" was translated from one Hebrew word, *bad*. It is made up of two Hebrew letters: vet and resh. These two letters combined mean the power of the mind. The definition of the Hebrew word *bad* is separated; apart, alone, solitary; divide. It does not mean against God! David separated himself from the Word, he was breaking faith, and he let his mind wander – and the mind is very powerful. Alone (separated from God) he sinned and sin took on an outward appearance – "done this evil in Thy sight." God was not to blame for David's sin and David acknowledged that – David did not play the blame game. He goes on in the next verse to say how *he* was "shapen in iniquity;" he knew the reason for his sin – it was his flesh. He knew he needed "purged with hyssop."

The definition of "purge" means to expiate or make up for, to cleanse or clean. We need to abide in what Christ has done for us – He has cleansed us from all of our sin. Connect with Him; walk in the forgiveness He paid for. This is how you start your new beginning.

Abide in the Word; be a disciple – be a student of the Word. We must know the difference between good and evil, between Spirit and flesh, just like David knew he was in sin because he was in his flesh and not yoked up to God. We must be able to divide soul and Spirit and we can only do that by abiding in the Word.

"Hyssop" has no definition but the meaning of the Hebrew letters that spell the Hebrew word for hyssop say it all…connect to Christ and receive His power. Abide in the Word – fasten yourself to it. This is how we turn things around!

David treated the Word with disrespect and let his flesh have control – can anyone relate? This trial was obviously brought about by him, so what did God do?

2 Samuel 12:13 (NIV) Then David said to Nathan, "I have sinned against the LORD." Nathan replied, "The LORD has taken away your sin. You are not going to die."

We do not have to feel imprisoned because of our sin. Nathan told David that the Lord had "taken away" his sin – this means to put away, to cross over, to cover, and to escape. Do not allow your sin to discourage you! When you are reminded of your sin, you must focus on the fact that you are forgiven! What Christ did for you made up for your sin – you have been purged!

> **Ezra 10:2 (NIV) Then Shecaniah son of Jehiel, one of the descendants of Elam, said to Ezra, "We have been unfaithful to our God by marrying foreign women from the peoples around us. But in spite of this, there is still hope for Israel."**

In Christ we always have hope and we need to be convinced of this. In spite of "this" – what is your "this?" No matter what your "this" is, there is still hope in Christ! This is not the end of your story; Christ has a new beginning in store and many great things to come! We simply must change our focus and look to Him.

> **Isaiah 55:7 (NIV) Let the wicked forsake his way and the evil man his thoughts. Let him turn to the LORD, and He will have mercy on him, and to our God, for He will freely pardon.**

The wages of sin is death. In the verses above dying is never mentioned as one of the consequences for his sin; yet, death is what God said David avoided. Death is an absence of the Spirit – the Spirit is life.

In the story of the prodigal son, the prodigal's father described the son as dead (Luke 15:20-25). That is what we are when we are living separated from God – remember the Hebrew word *bad*? Once the son was back in the father's presence he was classified as alive again! When we separate ourselves from the Father we are putting ourselves in a dead place; a place where only the flesh is at work. This son was just like David – David separated himself and found himself in a dead place, but God in His mercy imparted life to him again. The father was more concerned with *where* the son was than with *what* the son had done – if we are in the Spirit, then we will not fulfill the lusts of the flesh. Where are you? Are you in the Spirit or are you in your flesh?

Every Christian finds themselves in sin as the result of living outside the confines of the Word and we will *all* find ourselves in this predicament repeatedly. Sin is a daily conflict we all deal with; however, some sins are more obvious than others. In pointing out the sins of others we are taking the attention off of our own sin and many times that makes us more comfortable because we are not totally convinced of the forgiving power that is found in Christ. A need to draw attention to the sins of others is directly related to our inability to receive Christ's forgiveness for ourselves. If we meditate on the forgiveness that is found in the Word, then we will be set free from guilt and shame. The Word of God is our answer to every problem we may encounter and it is to our benefit to recognize this today!

The ultimate message of this book is to point out the benefits the Word of God bestows upon us in our day-to-day life. Seeing these benefits augments our desire to be in the Word, not because we are greedy and simply covet God's benefits, but because God puts in each one of us the desire to live the *Zoë* life that He has prepared for us. Even though this life of faith will be accompanied by the fight, I trust you have discovered that this fight is well worth the fighting.

Fight the good fight of faith; cling to the Word and be prepared for victory! The trial you are in is not the end – it is the beginning of all that God has in store for you! Fight for it!

WHY FIGHT?

As I write this book I am in a fight for my faith and I have asked myself the question posed in this chapter's title countless times. Why fight? Why go through this? Why do I have to go down the road quoting Scripture until tears flow down my face while the guy next to me jams to the radio and drinks his over-sized soda? Why is it that I cannot even clean my house without turning on a teaching CD because if I forget to turn it on my mind will wander and I will be consumed with the trials we are going through at the moment? Why is it that I try to figure all of this out over and over again but to what seems like no avail? Why is it that I beat myself up for feeling upset over my problems when other people have far greater things to deal with? Why is it? The list can go on. As I try to answer these questions and as I continue to go through these and many other situations like them, I can only conclude that God is in control and He works all things together for the good; I realize that does not *feel* like enough sometimes, but that is when I pray for my feelings to catch up with my Spirit and I run to the Word. It is not fun, it is not easy, and it is not always what I *want* to do. Many times I want to throw myself the world's biggest pity party, but that never helps; I know from experience! I know that this fight is arduous, but we have already looked at the fact that it is a *good* fight. I know we hate the struggle, but we also saw that Jesus Himself despised the shame. If Jesus despised the shame then I can, too! In the same way, if He endured the pain by looking to the joy set before Him, then I can also do the same because He lives in me!

"Why fight?" In the quest for the answer to this question, I find one answer in 2 Corinthians 2:14 – triumphal procession. Triumphal procession is motivation to fight. Triumphal procession is joy we can set before us. Who would not feel joy when they imagine victory, triumph, and conquest? Christ wants to parade you through the enemy's territory with the victory; that is joy set before you! The twenty-third Psalm tells us that He prepares a table for us in the presence of our enemies. Victory *is* ours and the devil *will* witness it and there will be nothing that he can do about it.

It is not easy to keep your mind set on visions of victory when you are in the heat of the battle, there is pain and Spiritual effort involved, but I have found that it is well worth the fight. I feel the pain you feel of going through something and seeing no end in sight. I know the throbbing heartache that comes along with wondering why God is not answering you. I am well aware of having your expectations disappointed only to have to get into the Word and start all over *again*. I appreciate how disheartening and frustrating it can all be, but understand that all of this is killing the one thing that is standing in the way of what we are fighting for. During this fight our flesh is dying little by little and every time we push past the pain of our flesh we are in essence declaring that our flesh means less to us than the Word of God. This is not about us, as long as we need an answer and as long as we need help, we only have one Source to go to. Each time we feel that our hopes are dashed yet we still reach for the Word to seek out more promises, we are crucifying our flesh. The flesh cries, "Give up! It will not happen for you! Don't you remember everything you have done?" Each time your flesh cries out you need to shout louder; shout the Word!

Tell your flesh who is boss; the Word of God is the boss in your life and your words verify that.

Keep in mind that trials are not a way of life; you are not meant to live in a perpetual trial, the trial is meant for a *little* while. You should be singing and enjoying your life; however, do not make the mistake of believing you cannot sing until your trial is over. Singing can lead us out of the trial. Singing can take us into a place of victory. As long as you find yourself in a place of testing keep your head up and keep your eyes on Christ, even when it seems impossible. Some days you may need to go to bed early and just start over fresh the next day, which is okay, too. We all have limits; that is why there are intermissions in a boxing match.

Remember that considering a trial pure joy does not mean we have to enjoy the pain. Despise the shame, endure the pain, and always keep the joy set before you so you can keep your focus on the Word of God instead of the trial.

It is not easy to fight for your faith. For me it has been painful, disturbing, and tempting, to name a few. My heart has felt broken, my faith has been stretched to "un-stretchable" measures in *my* opinion, and I have battled with the wrong thoughts on too many occasions, and yet the fight continues on! I have battled with feelings of failure. I have felt like giving up. Even now, when that thought of giving up enters my mind I am reminded of Peter's words.

John 6:68 (NIV)   Simon Peter answered Him, "Lord, to whom shall we go? You have the words of eternal life."

The option of giving up does not exist. Failure is Satan's lie. I have the Word of God and I have victory in His Word. Faith is the victory that overcomes everything and faith is the result of taking the Word in and making it part of who you are. I feel as if nothing is happening many times and there are even times when I feel like I am actually farther away from my blessing than the day before, but I must move forward in Christ. He is the only way for me to go; I have no other option.

If a circumstance in your life instigates doubt in you, then you can know that your faith is not genuine. I have criticized myself for possessing "counterfeit" faith during this fight and God has shown me the error in my ways – once again! Putting myself down did not trigger more living faith in my life; it continued to pull me down into my flesh. We must quickly recognize Satan's tricks. There will be times when our faith falls short of being genuine and during these times we must continue in the Word.

During this fight for our faith we must wrap ourselves in God's love. Love is being brought to my attention repeatedly. Perfect love casts out fear and fear is your enemy. Fear attacks relentlessly during the fight.

As we are waiting for God's Word to be established in our lives we are tempted to fear – fear that the promise will not come to pass for me, fear of what I will have to go through to see the promise, fear of my circumstances, and so on. Knowing that perfect love casts out fear, we must envelop ourselves with that love.

During this fight I feel like the author of Psalms. Many times the Psalms start out depressing and end up joyful. A Psalm may talk about defeat and discouragement in one verse and God's goodness in the next. Erratic is the description I can relate to. Fortunately, even when I am faithless He remains faithful. In my weakness He is made strong. We must take these unpredictable times and transform them into reasons to fight!

Why fight? Fight because God loves you and He has wonderful plans for you. Fight because God has already promised you the victory through Christ! Fight because God is worthy of our going into battle; we can fight believing every Word He has said because He is not a liar. Waging war against the enemy is our way of saying, "God, I believe You no matter what! I will go after everything You have promised me because I know that Your promises are one-hundred percent truth!" Fight on!

Stephanie White is a wife, mother, Bible teacher, and author. She enjoys spending time with her family and she is actively involved at her parents' church. She is passionate about sharing the Word of God with others so that they can live the life that Christ died to give them.

She loves to study the Word of God and share her studies with others. She has a website with monthly Bible studies, creative ideas for family and friends, date night ideas, and more.

https://whitestephanie83.wixsite.com/heavenonearthforyou

All Hebrew and Greek definitions are from the Strong's Hebrew and Greek dictionaries.

www.ingramcontent.com/pod-product-compliance
Lightning Source LLC
Chambersburg PA
CBHW051723040426
42447CB00008B/950